Atlantic Hazel
Scotland's Special Woodlands

Sandy and Brian Coppins
2012

'Discovery consists of seeing what everybody has seen
and thinking what nobody has thought.'

Albert von Szent-Györgyi 1893-1986, Hungarian biochemist

This project is the culmination of many years' exploration of Scotland's Atlantic hazel, initially by Brian Coppins and later with Sandy Coppins. The quotation above is very appropriate for Atlantic hazel and, hopefully, this publication will go some way to raising awareness of the unique and special qualities of the Atlantic hazelwood habitat, and will stimulate people to think beyond 'coppice'. We have benefited hugely from discussion and support from many people, but especially Andy Acton, Ben and Alison Averis, John Douglass, David Genney, the late Oliver Gilbert, Anna Griffith, Kate Holl, Joe Hope, Sharon Parr, Peter Quelch, the late Francis Rose, Neil Sanderson, Chris Smout, Gordon Gray Stephens and Stephen Ward.

A contract carried out on behalf of the Atlantic Hazel Action Group with funding from Scottish Natural Heritage, Argyll & the Islands EU Leader Programme and the British Lichen Society

Front cover: sunlight filtering through Atlantic hazel, Ballachuan Hazelwood, Scottish Wildlife Reserve, Seil, September 2010

Published by Atlantic Hazel Action Group
Old Poltalloch, Kilmartin, Argyll PA31 8RQ
01852 500366
info@atlantichazel.org

http://sites.google.com/site/atlantichazelgroup/

Atlantic Hazel Action Group (AHAG) is a partnership formed by organisations and individuals with an interest in Atlantic Hazelwoods.
Members include Argyll & Bute Biodiversity Partnership, British Lichen Society, Forestry Commission, Highland Biodiversity Partnership,
Plantlife, Scottish Natural Heritage, Scottish Wildlife Trust and individual lichenologists and consultants.

First published 2012

Design & layout: Helen Meek helen@ardessie.com
Printing: Big Sky Print Ltd www.bigskyprint.com

ISBN 978-0-9572034-0-2

Printed on FSC® Mix paper

MIX
Paper from
responsible sources
FSC® C020891
FSC
www.fsc.org

Abbreviations

BP: Before Present **HAP:** Habitat Action Plan **NNR:** National Nature Reserve **NVC:** National Vegetation Classification
SAF: Species Action Framework **SAP:** Species Action Plan **SSSI:** Site of Special Scientific Interest **SWT:** Scottish Wildlife Trust
PAWS: Plantation on Ancient Woodland Site

Foreword

By George Peterken

This book aims to change the way you think about hazel and in particular the hazel woods along the Atlantic seaboard. Until recently, most ecologists perceived hazel as just a coppiced shrub, the commonest component of the underwood in our widespread and enduring coppice-with-standards silvicultural system, and dismissed the hazel-dominated woods of the north and west as scrub - if they recognised them at all. Here, however, we are presented in a lavishly illustrated form with a more discriminating view, which sees the Atlantic hazel woods as a distinctive and highly significant type of woodland, the rain forest – no less – of the British Isles.

Like so many other ecologists, I have to plead guilty to a lowlander's view of hazel. I was well aware of hazel woods in western Scotland and Ireland, but I saw those on base-rich soils as attenuated forms of ash-elm woodland, which was itself a version of lime-ash-hazel woodland beyond the reach of lime. As to those on more acid substrates, I tended to assume they were versions of hazel-oak woodland from which the oak had probably been stripped. An analogy could also be drawn with birch and birch woodland, an opportunist species and a transitory type in the south, but increasingly dominant and longer-lived to the north and west where other trees reach their limits. The hazel woods could be fitted to larger patterns, but I thought of them as lesser forms of something else.

Here, the case is made for raising their profile. They are not only attractive and full of spring flowers, but full of unusual species, particularly the lichens, mosses and liverworts that thrive in an oceanic climate. They also seem to be survivors from the earliest woods to colonise Britain after the last ice age, protected on rough ground and by hazel's ability to sprout vigorously when it has the chance. By chance rather than design, these remnants allow us to appreciate not just one of our oldest environments, but one that is better represented here than elsewhere in Europe.

Important groups of woods have been almost ignored before. Lime woods do not appear in Tansley's *magnum opus*. Until the 1960s, we had difficulty recognising wood-pasture as a valid woodland type, to the extent that dense oak coppices established by planting were scheduled as SSSIs, while remnants of the older wood-pastures were ignored. Thanks in part to lichenologists, these have now been properly appreciated. No single book changed our thinking in this instance, but in the case of the Highland Scots pine woods it was *The Native Pinewoods of Scotland* that transformed our interest and eventually their prospects. The key seems to be coining a name, conferring an identity and at the same time increasing our understanding, thereby increasing public and professional interest and fostering a greater willingness to look after the survivors. Much the same has happened in other fields: by coining 'rhos pastures', for example, a distinctive form of wet grassland has emerged into the limelight and has become something we can identify, discuss and cherish.

This book will, I hope, put oceanic hazel woods on the map, greatly enlarge the number of people who will take an interest and promote a greater willingness to look after those that survive.

Contents

Carl Farmer

Above & right: Ben Averis

Introduction

What is 'Atlantic hazel'? It is hazel that occurs in the oceanic areas of the western British Isles. But, it is more than that. Hazel occurs widely all down the west side of Britain and Ireland, but only in a very few places does it achieve particular characteristics that mark it out as a distinctive habitat of high value for biodiversity. You know, when you step into an Atlantic hazelwood in Argyll, that this is somehow 'different'; you are struck by the greenness, the lushness, the strangeness of a dwarf wood. This is part of the 'Celtic rainforest'. So many hazel stems confuse the eye. In summer it is dark, shady and sheltered; the only light to filter down to the woodland floor through the dense canopy of hazel leaves is a green light. Mosses abound, forming thick carpets and cushions over rocks and on leaning branches, muffling sound and making it feel damp and cool, even when outside the sun is shining. If it is one of those 'typical' Argyll days, with dark clouds and rain, then it can be really dark and wet in an Atlantic hazelwood – and be a haven for midges. You can smell leaf-mould, and the fresh, green wetness of mosses. Ferns are found here, too, and if you look carefully, dark-hued, leafy-lobed lichens can be seen growing over mosses on branches and rocks. Atlantic hazelwoods are home to some of the richest assemblages of oceanic mosses, liverworts and lichens in the whole of Europe.

An Atlantic hazelwood in summer, on a steep, east-facing slope at South Screapadal, on Raasay, 2009. The stand appears deeply shaded, the closed canopy in full leaf, making the interior dark but very sheltered – a secret place. Areas of hazel like this occur in many places in western Scotland, but somehow they never quite achieve recognition as something that is very special to Scotland.

David Genney

A mosaic of crustose lichens on hazel at Loch a'Mhuilinn, 2004.

Yet Atlantic hazelwoods can also be a light and airy habitat, where the hazel stems are slender and the smooth bark is mottled with pale mosaics: silvery-white, cream, russet, grey and green. These are the small lichens, the crustose species that form thin, colourful mosaics over the surface of smooth hazel bark. Here, the air passes freely around the stems and bushes. Mosses are mostly found low down on the stems, or forming a thin carpet on the ground. When it rains, the rain slides down the stems, over the crustose lichens and soaks into the mossy 'socks', and when the rain stops, the stems dry very quickly. These lichens include some of the real specialities of the Atlantic hazelwoods, with a few not occurring anywhere else in the world.

Spring hazel cup, Ballachuan Hazelwood, Argyll, 2005.

Hazel gloves, Tokavaig, Isle of Skye, 2007.

> It would be a tragedy to lose Scottish Atlantic hazelwoods through lack of knowledge and misguided management.

Atlantic hazel at South Screapadal, Raasay, 2009. The hazel here is growing as a pure stand, not as an understorey shrub. It is naturally multi-stemmed and has never been coppiced. It is a stand of ancient woodland.

Atlantic hazelwoods are also home to some fascinating and beautiful fungi, such as spring hazel cup *Encoelia furfuracea* and the particularly curious hazel gloves *Hypocreopsis rhododendri*. The latter is a very rare fungus and seems to occur only in Atlantic hazelwoods that are believed to be ancient woodlands.

The bryophytes (mosses and liverworts), the large, leafy-lobed lichens, the small crustose lichens, the ferns and the fungi are all part of what makes Atlantic hazelwoods a special habitat. In spring, before the hazel leaves open out, the catkins make a delightful show and the flowers can be really spectacular. But surprisingly little is known or written about Atlantic hazelwoods, and as a habitat it receives very little attention, or even recognition. The Atlantic hazelwoods of western Scotland deserve to be more widely appreciated and recognised as a unique and important habitat in a European and world context.

This publication aims to:
- Describe why Atlantic hazelwoods form a distinct habitat of high conservation value.
- Highlight why many well-meaning misconceptions about hazel, and its management requirements, put this internationally important habitat and the species it supports at considerable risk.
- Provide guidance to assess whether a hazel stand is in 'good' condition, and to offer advice on management.

Currently, very few Atlantic hazelwoods fall within protected areas, so most are vulnerable to poor management because they are outside the focus of current agri-environment schemes and grants for sympathetic and supportive management.

Some universally held beliefs about hazel that are not true, and are the hardest to shake off

Hazel is familiar to everybody, and is one of the commonest woody species throughout the British Isles. Yet, it appears to be the least studied, the least understood, and generally the most overlooked. There are a few myths and misconceptions about hazel that may well encourage well meaning but inappropriate management that could threaten the nature and diversity of this special west-coast Atlantic Hazelwood habitat. The following statements are generally held to be true by most people, including those interested in wildlife and woodland history, by most woodland ecologists, by woodland managers and by conservationists.

Hazel misconceptions
- **Hazel occurs naturally as an understorey shrub**
- **Multi-stemmed hazel is all hazel coppice**
- **Hazel will die out if it is not regularly coppiced**
- **Hazel will develop into a single-trunked tree if left uncoppiced**

None of these statements is true, especially of Atlantic hazel. The following pages will demonstrate that hazel is not 'naturally' an understorey shrub, and that hazel grows 'naturally' as a multi-stemmed shrub, quite independent of any intervention by man, and certainly without being coppiced. Hazel will die out where it is left to weaken gradually under increasing shade of tall trees. Hazel 'trees' may develop when hazel has been subjected to extended periods of intensive grazing, but when the grazing is removed the trees will quickly revert back to multi-stemmed shrubs.

There is a real need to stop, look and think again about hazel, especially the wonderful, ancient, species-rich Atlantic hazelwoods.

Some of the biodiversity of Atlantic hazelwoods

Ben Averis; David Genney; Liz Holden; Gordon Rothero; Sandy Coppins

> **Atlantic hazelwoods are some of Scotland's most ancient woodlands. They are older by far than the Atlantic oakwoods of Scotland, and older than some of the Caledonian pinewoods.**

Hazel *Corylus avellana* was one of the first woody species to establish along the western edge of Scotland as the ice retreated, some 11,000 years ago (Birks 1989; Tallantire 2002). The pollen evidence also suggests that pure hazel scrub dominated vast areas of western Scotland for perhaps a thousand years (Birks 1989; McVean 1964). Today, remnant stands of pure hazel (with no tall trees) are still a feature in some places, especially in coastal areas of the western Scottish Highlands, suggesting a continuous presence of an ancient habitat for nearly 10,000 years (Birks 1989).

The pollen evidence suggests that, after the ice retreated, hazel first moved into the British Isles from south-west Ireland and across to the western seaboard of north Wales, Anglesey, north-west England, Isle of Man, up to Antrim in north-eastern Ireland, across to Dumfries and Galloway, up to Kintyre, Islay, Jura, then up the western edge of Argyll (including the Sleat Peninsula on Skye), Wester Ross and on to Caithness. This is a fascinating dispersal pattern (see map). To some extent, interpretation in the map is constrained by sampling sites (hence the broken demarcation line in places), but the shaded areas strongly suggest that hazel was distributed by nuts floating on sea currents, which were washed into sheltered inlets all along the western coasts of Wales, northern England and Scotland, and along the coastal edges of north-eastern Ireland. The more exposed shores and islands, where flotsam was not deposited by currents issuing up from the Irish Sea, did not get hazelnuts quite as soon. The one sampling site on the Outer Hebrides found hazel pollen to be absent, which is intriguing.

There are some suggestions that perhaps there was a land-bridge between Ireland and western Britain, and that hazel migrated across from Ireland when sea-levels were lower. However, the hypothesis of water transport seems to be the most widely accepted.

So, do hazelnuts float? Yes, most definitely. *(See box opposite).*

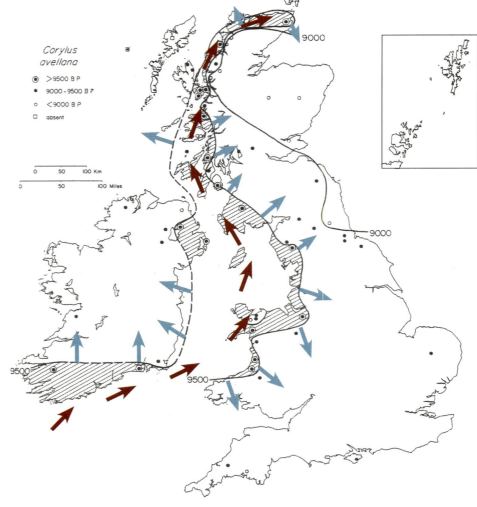

Corylus avellana
- ◉ >9500 B P
- ● 9000 - 9500 B P
- ○ <9000 B P
- □ absent

The approximate area (shaded) where hazel was present earlier than 9,500 years Before Present (BP). Suggested primary (red arrows) and secondary (blue arrows) colonisation routes are also shown. The map is based on the distribution of hazel pollen in sediments aged by radiocarbon dating (sites shown as dots) (Birks 1989).

Cathir Chomáin, Co. Clare, October 2008. Parts of the Burren, in south-west Ireland, are extensively covered with dense stands of hazel over the limestone, sometimes (as here) for as far as the eye can see. This clearly shows that hazel is a pioneering species, and will successfully invade open ground. Although there are some 'core' old-growth areas, there has been a fairly recent dramatic expansion of hazel in Co. Clare as a result of changes in farming practices. Apart from the landscape here being gently undulating, is this how the early post-glacial landscape would have looked in western Scotland?

Do hazelnuts float?

A bowl of hazelnuts, autumn 2009. These were actually harvested from the **filbert** *Corylus maxima* (from bushes at Dunbar, south-east Scotland). The nuts are slightly larger than wild **common hazel** *C. avellana*. However, for purposes of testing whether hazelnuts float, these are perfectly acceptable.

The hazelnuts were tipped into a trough of rainwater and all floated, both the nuts with papery bracts and those without. Several days later, the nuts were taken out to dry and were cracked open to reveal good, tasty kernels.

This little experiment, of course, does not provide conclusive evidence that hazelnuts will float and remain viable for extended periods in seawater.
However, this could provide the basis for an interesting project for schools in the west coast of Scotland.

Sunlight filtering down through the canopy of an Atlantic hazelwood – part of Ballachuan Hazelwood, a Scottish Wildlife Trust Reserve, Argyll, September, 2010. This is a site of high biodiversity, of international importance for its lichens. The woodland occupies 23 ha of almost pure hazel. It is an 'ancient woodland' in that it is believed to be a relic dating back to the retreat of the last ice age. This hazel has not been coppiced. It maintains its multi-stem form quite naturally.

‘Hazel is essentially a light-demanding, pioneer species that will invade open ground and form self-perpetuating, pure, dense stands that can persist indefinitely, despite some grazing, and certainly in the absence of coppicing.’

An unrecognised or misunderstood habitat

Although this habitat has been with us for thousands of years, the Atlantic hazelwoods do not fit comfortably into any of the British National Vegetation Classification (NVC) community types (Rodwell 1991), nor are they recognised in their own right by the European Habitats Directive, the legislation that gives some of the strongest protection to habitats and species. Many misunderstandings have arisen about the nature of hazel, mainly influenced by the way that hazel has been intensively managed since early medieval times in lowland England. Coppice-with-standards was a traditional form of management that gave the maximum yield from carefully husbanded lowland woodlands in England. Hazel was the 'coppice', regularly cut every seven or so years, as the highly valued 'underwood' product. Hazel was interspersed with standard trees, such as oak or ash, grown for their larger-dimension timber. Over many centuries, these traditions have become ingrained in the way woodland managers regard hazel, as the understorey shrub to woodland trees. Books on woodland ecology that form the basis for our understanding and appreciation of woodland processes and the way trees behave have mainly emanated from lowland England, and have largely perpetuated these views.

One of the most accepted aspects of woodland ecology is that hazel is an **understorey shrub**. However this is clearly not the case in exposed coastal areas of western Scotland and Ireland.

Sir Arthur Tansley, a leading ecologist of the first half of the 20th century, offered a challenge to the accepted wisdom of hazel being an understorey shrub to taller trees after his visit to the Burren, in south-west Ireland. He recognised the vast hazel-scrub habitat as being, in fact, a 'climax' community that would never become over-topped by taller tree species (Tansley 1949).

More recently, the influential woodland ecologist Oliver Rackham has clearly demonstrated that hazel is not a natural understorey shrub (Rackham 2003). He describes the effects that shading – being over-topped by taller trees – has on hazel. It causes it to become drawn up and leggy. With increased shade from surrounding trees, hazel vigour is slowed down or arrested, with the loss of many stems from the base, and with the remaining stems managing only a slow thickening over a period of perhaps 50 years. **Hazel never flowers or produces nuts whilst under shade from over-topping trees**. Under a well-regulated

'We'd better hurry up, or hazel will never reach Scotland'

This cartoon by Ben Averis depicts prehistoric woodcutters desperately coppicing hazel before it dies out, in order for it to reach Scotland. Clearly an impossible task! We now accept that hazel – pure stands of hazel – dominated the landscape of the Atlantic edges of Scotland for many thousands of years, and that presumed relics of this ancient woodland are still persisting today. Coppicing of hazel was probably only ever a very marginal management activity in the oceanic woodlands. The habitat was so widespread that selective cutting of required stems easily satisfied demand.

coppice-with-standards management regime, hazel vigour is maintained. In lapsed coppice, hazel is gradually dying out (Rackham 2003). The benefits of 're-coppicing' to invigorate the hazel stools is seen as the answer to save the hazel, and hazel does respond very positively to being coppiced. Thinning overgrown standard trees and removing the old hazel canopy allows light to reach the coppiced stools, and this stimulates new growth. However, Rackham qualifies the benefits of coppicing, acknowledging that it is purely a management device:

> ❝This process does not apply to woods in which hazel has only other hazels to compete with. **Coppicing has not created hazelwoods**, which have existed throughout prehistory, but it has enabled hazel to be commoner in mixtures than it would otherwise be.❞
>
> Rackham 2003

The 'hazel-coppice' mind-set

Today, the widespread belief that all multi-stemmed hazel stools are the result of past coppicing is a notion that is hard to change.

- Literature searches on the ecology of hazel reveal little about hazel per se. When hazel is mentioned, it is dismissed at best as 'scrub' or 'understorey', or (the universal favourite) 'hazel-coppice', and at worst (and no matter where the hazel stand occurs) as 'neglected hazel-coppice'.

- Hazel does lend itself admirably to being coppiced, and the uses to which coppiced hazel has been put over the centuries are many and varied.

- The biodiversity benefits of **regularly maintained** coppice are known to include herb-rich ground floras, and coppicing can support a high diversity of insects and birds. Coppicing, in effect, creates a series of temporary woodland glades. It is not surprising then, that management of hazel as coppice is elaborately described in glowing terms in all books on woodland management. Hence, students and woodland managers are swayed into thinking that this is the way hazel has always been, and should be, managed, and that all stands of hazel, wherever they occur, are automatically regarded as 'hazel-coppice'.

- Some woodland ecologists believe that hazel will die out if it is not regularly coppiced and 'reinvigorated'. As Rackham (2003) observed, this is certainly the fate of hazel that was formerly part of a coppice-with-standards regime, where today it is, indeed, 'neglected hazel-coppice', weakened by being over-topped and shaded out. This scenario is most often encountered in the woodlands of lowland England. However, in upland Britain – and especially in the Atlantic coastal woods of western Scotland, where hazel forms pure stands and is not over-topped by dense tree canopy – hazel forms a self-perpetuating habitat that appears to be able to persist indefinitely, and certainly in the absence of coppicing.

What's in a name?

Distribution of hazel and its cousins

- Hazel is found in temperate zones of Europe and western Asia, and only the **common hazel** *Corylus avellana* is native to the British Isles. Our native hazel occurs throughout the British Isles, being absent only from the high mountains and the bogs of the Flow Country (Preston *et al*. 2002).

- Of the 15 species of hazel found throughout the northern hemisphere, only one grows naturally with a tree-like stature from a single trunk, the **Turkish hazel** *Corylus colurna*. This grows to 20m or more, and is a native of south-east Europe and south-west Asia. It was introduced to Britain and is occasionally planted as a street tree (e.g. in London, on the Embankment by Blackfriars Bridge), or as an ornamental park tree (e.g. in the grounds of Bristol Zoo). The rest, like the common hazel, are multi-stemmed shrubs.

- Other non-native hazels found in Britain include the **filbert** *Corylus maxima*, which is cultivated, especially in Kent, to produce the Kentish cobnut (larger than the common hazelnut).

- Unusual hazels found in ornamental parks and gardens include a cultivar of *Corylus avellana* 'Contorta' (the corkscrew hazel, also known as Harry Lauder's Walking Stick), and the purple-leaved hazel 'Purpurea', which is a cultivar of *C. maxima*.

Hazel in Gaelic, calltunn/calltuinn

The scientific name is *Corylus avellana* L. This was the name given to the shrub by Linnaeus in the 18th century. He selected the name from Leonhart Fuch's *De historia stirpium commentarii insigness* (1542), where the species was described as '*Avellana nux sylvestris*' (or, 'the wild nut of the forest of Avella', Avella being a town in Italy, sylvestris meaning 'of the forest').

http://en.wikipedia.org/wiki/Corylus_avellana

Hazel leaves. Ben Averis

Atlantic hazel *Corylus avellana*, in the lushness of full summer leaf. This is part of Ballachuan Hazelwood, on Seil, Argyll, 2010.

Description of Hazel
Corylus avellana

Hazel is a multi-stemmed shrub, i.e. there is more than one stem arising from the rootstock, in the healthy plant. It is essentially a pioneering, light-demanding shrub, so one of the requirements for successful germination and establishment is that there is no closed canopy above to shade out the emerging seedling. Seedlings germinate from the previous autumn's nuts. Initially, a single stem will arise, soon to be joined by other stems, and in 5-10 years it forms a characteristic small, multi-stemmed and branching hazel shrub. Seedlings are palatable to most herbivores, from voles through to sheep, cattle, ponies and deer. However, once established, and depending on the situation, a typical multi-stemmed hazel shrub can reach in excess of 10m in height, although most hazel bushes tend to be between 3m and 5m high. There are examples of very exposed, wind-pruned hazels that form dwarf stands

A typical multi-stemmed hazel at Loch a'Mhuilinn Site of Special Scientific Interest, West Sutherland, 2004. This hazel is inside a recently fenced exclosure. The prolific young basal regeneration is not browsed, and is growing rapidly to reach the canopy, so increasing the viable number of stems.

Top: Loch a'Mhuilinn SSSI, West Sutherland, 2004. Regeneration within an exclosure. Although birch is establishing in discrete patches, there is a mass of hazel regeneration. Bottom: Loch a'Mhuilinn, 2004. Detail of natural hazel regeneration in well-lit, open conditions. Regeneration is from nuts of nearby established hazels.

Hazel bark

Glen Nant National Nature Reserve, Argyll, May 2010. Young stems of hazel have smooth bark. In Atlantic hazelwoods, this is colonised by a range of crustose lichens (including some species given priority for conservation action under the UK Biodiversity Action Plan), which form pale-coloured, closed mosaics over the surface of the bark.

Above and left: Smooth hazel bark at Tyninghame, East Lothian, January 2010.

The lichen interest on these hazels is extremely low, to almost absent. It is likely that the stand may have been coppiced in the past. However, comparing these East Lothian hazels with those in western Scotland, the difference in overall biodiversity for bryophytes and lichens is immediately obvious.

Co. Fermanagh, Northern Ireland, April 2010. Young and maturing Atlantic hazel stems. Note the smooth bark with crustose lichen mosaics, and slightly roughened bark where bryophytes are establishing. The very young stem in the centre is quick-growing and splitting apart the outer membranous skin. The larger stem on the right has suffered bark-stripping damage by feral goats.

Lochcarron, Wester Ross, 2003. Characteristically, these old Atlantic hazel stems support bryophytes and a profusion of lichens where the bark has become roughened and fissured, trapping moisture.

Hazel catkins

In early spring, before the leaves appear, **male catkins** ('lambs-tails') develop. The catkins produce conspicuous pale yellow pollen that is wind-dispersed, and dancing hazel catkins are a characteristic sight early in the year, shedding pollen into the spring air.

A series of pictures of west-coast hazel, March 2010. The catkins make hazel stand out at this time of the year (early spring). The catkins elongate and change colour as they mature. When the sun strikes a hazel full of catkins, the result can be a mass of flaming gold or silver, there for a day or two and then gone till next year.

Gordon Gray Stephens

'Today I saw the catkins blow
Altho' the hills are white with snow;
While throstles sang "The sun is good",
They waved their banners in the wood.
They came to greet the lurking spring
As messengers from winter's King.'

'February' Dorothy Una Ratcliffe

Arduaine, Argyll, March 2010. Gordon Gray Stephens

David Genney

The **female flowers** are mostly overlooked because of the showy male catkins. They occur on the same branch as the male catkins, and are small, squat, reddish buds ('the dwarfy females'). They have neat tufts of 12 crimson styles, which catch the pollen.

A female flower with tuft of crimson styles. Pollination of hazel is by wind, and fertilisation only takes place between different shrubs (a hazel cannot pollinate itself). After fertilisation, a new twig develops from the base of the flower, carrying the developing nuts and new leaves.

Note also the glandular hairs on the twigs, characteristic of the young winter-spring twigs of hazel. See:

http://www.plant-identification.co.uk/skye/ for further hazel photographs.

Leaves and nuts

Hazel **leaves** are fairly large (up to 10cm x 10cm), oval, with serrated double-toothed edges and a pointed tip. There is a rough feel to the upper side of the leaf as it is covered with short hairs; the underside is paler, with soft, whitish hairs on the veins. Hazel **stems** bear alternate buds, giving the twig a slightly angular look.

The nuts are encased in strong, papery sheaths (bracts). Young nuts are pale green, changing to ivory and eventually to brown. The hard shell encloses a single seed or kernel.

Nuts are not produced every year as fruiting depends on several factors, such as the spring weather, notably incidence of late frosts. Nuts are most often found on well-lit bushes in relatively warm, sheltered situations. Hazel growing under the canopy of tall trees very rarely flowers or sets seed.

Young, developing hazelnuts. Portree, Isle of Skye, July, 2004.

A cluster of ripe hazelnuts. Portree, Isle of Skye, early November.

Hazelnuts are an important food source for a whole range of animals and birds. For example, in western Scotland field voles, wood mice, great spotted woodpeckers and great tits feed on hazelnuts. Red squirrels are rare in the west, and bank voles are scattered there, but both are known to feed on hazelnuts. Several mammals will gather hazelnuts and cache them as a source of winter food. It has been suggested that some mammals (e.g. field voles) will gather hazelnuts from a wood, and cache them away in open grassland, thus assisting the spread of hazel. Other small mammals will create caches of nuts within the woodland; some of these nuts could lie uneaten over the winter and, come the spring, may germinate to create new hazel bushes intertwined with the roots of existing bushes – presenting a challenging scenario to those considering investigating the genetics of hazel *Corylus avellana* in an old-growth Atlantic hazelwood.

Typical caches of hazelnuts under old hazels within Atlantic hazelwoods. These are wood-mice caches, although other herbivores have ransacked the hoards.

Top: Co. Fermanagh; bottom: hazelwood on Isle of Luing, Argyll, both spring 2010.

This cache of hazelnuts was dug out in January 2006, in Ballachuan Hazelwood, SWT Reserve, Isle of Seil. Sometimes these nut hoards are not refound, and this can lead to the nuts germinating and forming new hazel bushes, close under the root-stool of an existing hazel.

Detail of the unearthed nut hoard, showing how the field mouse has gnawed sections out of the nutshells to reach the nutritious kernel. Field mice, voles, squirrels and woodpeckers all leave distinctive 'trademarks' on a hazelnut as they break open the shell.

Defining an Atlantic Hazelwood

Habitat edge. Ballachuan Hazelwood, SWT Reserve, 2005.

Scrub or woodland?

Should stands of Atlantic hazel be termed 'scrub' or 'woodland'?

'Scrub' used to be a dismissive, derogatory term, often indicating a secondary habitat of low value, but more recently the wildlife value of scrub has been recognised, resulting in it being reassessed as an important habitat in its own right (Mortimer et al. 2000). The term 'scrub' covers a whole range of habitats, in both uplands and lowlands, but mostly people think of **'scrub' as bushes or stunted trees, woody vegetation generally less than 5m tall (but not including dwarf shrubs, such as heather)**. Expressions such as 'a bit of scrubby woodland' describing an area of poorly developed, stunted or scrappy tree or shrub regeneration often sound derogatory.

'Scrub' is also often taken to be a seral stage, being a transition from open, herbaceous vegetation to woodland (**seral scrub**, or 'something that will turn into a proper wood given time'). And it is generally assumed that most modern scrub is almost entirely a result of man's activities.

However, there are exceptions, in that there are **natural types of scrub**, although these are very rare. Some scrub is recognised as forming a climax vegetation community (i.e. it will always stay as 'scrub'), although this is usually understood to be as a result of certain restrictions on the development of the woody plants, such as cold and exposure (alpine and sub-alpine zones), exposed, wind-blasted coasts, or thin skeletal soils, or combinations of several of these.

Hazel stands occurring along some parts of the west coast of Scotland and Ireland form **climax scrub**; this is **scrub that has persisted, and will continue to do so, indefinitely under the current climate**, and not become infiltrated by taller trees and develop into woodland. Hazel-dominated landscapes appear to have existed in these localities from as long ago as 10,000 years (Birks 1989), mostly along the coastal fringes where exposure and thin soils over rocky or steep slopes have largely prevented the establishment of other woody species.

Hazel scrub today usually forms dense, compact stands, the twigs forming a closed canopy, so that within the stand it is relatively sheltered, yet in summer, when in full leaf, it is shaded and dark. Under these conditions, it is almost impossible for other trees to establish.

Can hazel scrub persist indefinitely?

Hazel possesses a unique advantage over other forms of scrub, such as hawthorn and blackthorn. Although hawthorn and blackthorn can form closed stands – thickets where no other tree species can penetrate – both these shrubs arise from a single trunk. As the canopies expand and close over, the lower canopy is shaded, branches here begin to die off, and the centre of the stand assumes a leggy structure. Eventually, individual old bushes die off, and provide regeneration opportunities for trees to establish (assuming tree seed sources are readily available) before the surrounding shrubs regenerate into the space. **But hazel, being a multi-stemmed shrub, can constantly be replenished, thereby not relying on the lifespan of the single trunk, the stand can be a structural continuum**.

Significant stands of Atlantic hazel are usually described as **hazel woodland** (e.g. Ballachuan Hazelwood, Scottish Wildlife Trust Reserve, on the Isle of Seil, Argyll, is 23ha of almost pure hazel). Walking into one of the long-established, ancient hazel 'woods', the ground flora certainly suggests that this is a 'woodland', with spring flowers such as primroses, wood anemones and bluebells, together with dog's mercury. The bryophyte, lichen and fungal biodiversity would also suggest that this is **an ancient woodland habitat**.

Large patches of hazel that have recently invaded or expanded, for example the huge expanses of hazel covering the limestone areas on the Burren, in Co. Clare, Ireland, and similar but less extensive areas on the limestone in Co. Fermanagh, Northern Ireland, are usually described as **hazel scrub**. Small patches of hazel on hillsides, or at the edges of other woodland, are also sometimes referred to as 'bits of scrubby hazel'.

Although pure stands of hazel are, strictly speaking, **scrub**, the term 'hazel woodland', as used here, refers to old-growth woodland, a distinctive habitat apparently unique to western Scotland. To distinguish it clearly, it is further defined as Atlantic hazel woodland.

Wind-sculptured hazel canopy at Ballachuan, Argyll.

Sir Arthur Tansley

Sir Arthur Tansley was a highly respected 20th century ecologist. He recognised what he termed 'climax scrub', stands of scrub on windswept and exposed situations, or where certain soil conditions prevent the growth of trees, but are able to support shrubs (Tansley 1949). Climax scrub occurs on exposed coastal sites and in some upland localities. Tansley used as an example significant stands of closed hazel found on thin soils over the limestone of the Burren, Co. Clare, in western Ireland. Here, under a hyperoceanic climate, is a windswept, exposed landscape of extensive, horizontal limestone beds, rising in a series of low terraces. Thick hazel scrub has developed in the sheltered lee of low cliffs at the edge of terraces, and forms considerable stands. In more sheltered conditions adjacent to the small cliffs, the hazel canopy reaches 3m in height, but at the wind-exposed edges the canopy height is restricted to 60-90cm, and projecting canopy twigs are contorted or killed from exposure to severe winds. Examples of similar closed-canopy stands of pure hazel can also be found at scattered localities along the coasts of western Scotland (e.g. Mull, Islay, Skye, Eigg, Morvern, Ardnamurchan), with more inland examples further north at Inverpolly and Assynt.

A hazel 'tree' in a sheltered glade at Loch a'Mhuilinn SSSI, West Sutherland, 2005, created through long-term grazing pressure. The 'trunk' is mossy and almost completely covered in tree lungwort *Lobaria pulmonaria*. At the base are small shoots that are being browsed off by deer. With a reduction of grazing pressure, these basal shoots would fully develop and this hazel would revert to a multi-stemmed shrub.

Is hazel a tree or a shrub?

Although both 'tree' and 'shrub' have been applied to hazel, the definition of '**tree**' as supplied by www.answers.com/topic/tree is: '(a) a perennial woody plant having a main trunk and usually a distinct crown; (b) a plant or shrub resembling a tree in form or size.' On the same website, the Columbia Encyclopaedia states:

'tree, perennial woody plant with a single main stem (the trunk, or bole) from which branches and twigs extend to form a characteristic crown of foliage. In general, a tree differs from a shrub in that it has a single trunk, it reaches a greater height at maturity, it branches at a greater distance from the ground, and it increases in size by producing new branches and expanding in girth while a shrub often produces new shoots from ground level.'

The term 'tree' has been used for hazel, although strictly speaking it is a '**shrub**'. Hazel 'trees' are known to exist, but these are almost always created as a result of the long exposure of the hazel to constant grazing, whereby the natural growth form of many stems arising from the rootstock has been thwarted. They are found in upland wood pasture, as well as in grazed woodlands.

Hazel 'trees'

In all instances, these arose as a result of long periods of grazing around the base of the hazel, reducing this to a single stem that carried the canopy above grazing height. Each spring, new shoots are put up at the base of the trunk but are browsed off, leading to a gradual thickening of the hazel 'trunk'.

In some instances, this has resulted in a thickened swelling at the base, giving some indication of the extreme age of some of these hazel 'trees'. Removal of grazing would result in most cases in the 'trees' reverting to multi-stemmed shrubs.

Erray, Mull, 2000.

Loch a'Mhuilinn, 2004.

Glen Nant, 2010.

Glen Nant, 2010.

Exmoor, 1998.

Allt Rhyd y Groes, 1997.

The Atlantic hazel habitat

A 'pure' hazel stand is defined as a stand that is more than 75% hazel. Hazel can occur on basic to somewhat acidic soils (along with brambles, bluebells and bracken), and often on rocky ground with thin soils. In these situations it is usually small, stunted and compact, with a relatively quick turnover of stems within the small, close-packed bases. It can also be found on damp, deep loam soils, where it can exceed an amazing height of 15m, with many stems, and the individual hazels well spaced and achieving a significant girth (Rackham 2003).

The Atlantic hazelwood habitat is a self-perpetuating habitat, one that persists without being coppiced. It is believed that some sites may be ancient relics of the original 'wildwood'. What is the evidence for this, and how does hazel manage to persist as a viable habitat? Seeking to understand the dynamics of this fascinating habitat started with the study of lichens.

The lichen story

(text mostly taken from Coppins et al. 2002)

The story begins in the late 1970s, when Brian Coppins (senior lichenologist at the Royal Botanic Garden Edinburgh) started to look more closely at hazel as a host for lichens. It soon became clear that there was something special about the Atlantic hazelwood habitat compared with habitats with hazel stands elsewhere in the British Isles. The lichens of smooth hazel bark were particularly intriguing, with many unknown, yet distinctive, species. Subsequent study revealed that some of these were new to Britain or Europe, and others were new to science. However, even in the western Highlands and Islands, these 'new' species were not found everywhere on hazel. They were virtually absent from hazels under the canopies of oaks, and always absent from hazel stands that had developed from clear-cutting, or that had invaded open ground during the last 50-100 years (Coppins & Coppins 1999; Gilbert 1984).

The best hazels for lichens are found in woodlands where hazel forms the dominant canopy, on ridges and knolls or slopes close to the sea. Prime examples are found at Ballachuan Hazelwood SWT Reserve (on the Isle of Seil, Argyll), south of Drimnin (Morvern), Struidh Wood (on Eigg) and Resipole Ravine (Sunart).

When entering these hazelwoods, one is struck by the fact that the slender stems are not bare, but are covered with colourful mosaics of small crustose lichens.

Crustose lichens can appear as just smoothish pale-coloured patches, with perhaps warts or black dots scattered on the surface. Others have small lines like scribbles. It is this last group (the **'script' lichens**) that lends its name to this community of crustose lichens: the *Graphidion scriptae* (*Graphidion* for short).

The *Graphidion* community occurs worldwide, but in the British Isles comprises about 65 species, of which **about 20 can be considered specialists in that they are confined to Atlantic woodlands, especially hazelwoods**. A few also occur in western Scotland on other smooth-barked trees, such as rowan and holly.

Walking further into the hazelwood, the stand becomes more enclosed and sheltered, and more shady conditions prevail. The hazel stems (at least the older, thicker ones), have bryophytes occurring higher up the stem, and large, leafy-lobed lichens are often present. These include species of the genera Lobaria, Nephroma, Degelia, Pseudocyphellaria, Sticta, Pannaria and Leptogium, all members of the Lobarion community. **All these lichens are today very rare and declining elsewhere in Europe, so Scotland has an International Responsibility for lichens of the Lobarion** (Woods & Coppins 2003).

Smooth-barked Atlantic hazel at Dundonnell, Wester Ross, 2008, with crustose lichen mosaics, including *Pyrenula macrospora*.

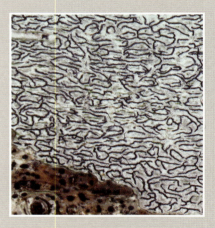

Two typical 'script' lichens characteristic of the smooth bark of Atlantic hazelwoods: (above) *Graphis scripta*, with elongated, sinuous 'scribble', a widespread hazel lichen, and (below) *Melaspilea atroides*, tiny, contorted scribbles, and a real Atlantic hazelwood specialist, known from Kintyre north to Assynt. Elsewhere in the British Isles, there are only a few records of this species from north Wales (Merioneth), and western Ireland (Killarney, Connemara and Donegal).

Atlantic hazel at Ballachuan Hazelwood, SWT Reserve, Seil, Argyll, 2005. Typical stand on sloping, fairly shallow soil. The hazels with medium to slender stems maintain a closed canopy through constant replenishment of young stems replacing old. A magical place.

Yellow specklebelly *Pseudocyphellaria crocata*. Lochcarron, Wester Ross, 2003.

Tree lungwort *Lobaria pulmonaria*, Dundonnell, Wester Ross, 2008.

One of the 'specialists' is apparently endemic to Scotland: the **white script lichen** *Graphis alboscripta* has not been found outside the core Atlantic hazelwoods of Western Scotland. Several of the Graphidion lichens are BAP (**Biodiversity Action Plan**) species, and are undergoing study to understand their present status. They are also of **International Importance** in a European, and in some cases, world context.

Defining an Atlantic hazelwood site

To qualify as a site, the minimum seems to be 50 individual hazels in order to form a distinctive and recognisable Atlantic hazelwood habitat. This is greater than the minimum stand size for recognising the aspen priority habitat, where the presence of one aspen is considered the baseline. However, aspen is significantly rarer in Scotland than hazel, so direct comparison is not applicable. Even this criterion can present problems, such as how to calculate roadside strips of hazel, some of which are known to support significant *Graphidion* communities. The distinction of 50 hazels forming the minimum site must be seen as a guide only.

The minimum size is unlikely to support all typical biodiversity features associated with larger stands, but even so, small stands or groups of hazel will provide a kernel of a habitat. In the Atlantic climatic zone, even small groups of hazel will almost certainly have bryophytes, fungi and lichens not found on other trees or shrubs within a site, and so contribute positively to the overall wildlife interest. Managers should consider management that will maintain and expand existing stands, while at the same time enhancing the ecological condition of the Atlantic hazelwood habitat, and should expand the area only where this can be done without compromising adjacent semi-natural habitats.

Suitable management is discussed below. It often involves conservation grazing (see www.forestry.gov.uk/ woodlandgrazingtoolbox)

The distinction between what we consider as the ancient, relict habitat of the true Atlantic hazelwoods and other stands of hazel scattered throughout much of lowland western Scotland is a difficult line to draw. There is a lot of blurring at the edges. Atlantic hazel can occur as remote, wind-clipped coastal woodland; as small to large stands adjacent to (or even within) other woodlands; as mosaics and woodland corridors; as scattered, linear remnants alongside roads; or as isolated, remnant clumps under rocky outcrops, amongst bouldery slopes, within commercial forestry, or along streams.

At present, the **main evidence for a relict hazelwood appears to lie with the lichens**, particularly the incidence of species within the western group of the *Graphidion*. There are, at this stage, more questions than answers; much more work needs to be devoted to the ecology of hazelwoods. Fortunately, one does not have to be a

Scattered hazel flanking semi-natural woodland edge to a large, open bracken field. These hazels provide valuable habitat diversity at this sunny, sheltered spot in Taynish NNR, Argyll.

Peter Quelch

Hazel gloves. Tokavaig, Isle of Skye, December 2007.

lichen 'expert' in order to make an initial assessment of any particular stand of hazel, as the hazel gloves fungus can provide a relatively easy entrée as a distinctive and easily recognisable 'flagship' species.

Hazel gloves *Hypocreopsis rhododendri* is given priority for conservation action by the UK Biodiversity Action Plan (UKBAP) and Scottish Natural Heritage's Species Action Framework (SAF)[1]. As well as being a priority species in its own right (Nationally rare, present in less than 16 10km squares in the UK), **hazel gloves is also a good indicator of potentially species-rich Atlantic hazelwoods**.

However, absence of hazel gloves **does not imply** that the hazel stand is likely to be of low interest. Hazel gloves has a limited distribution, and does not appear 'in fruit' every year, even at known sites. **Hazel Attribute Tables (HATs) are included in Appendix 1** of this booklet, to enable easy assessment of stands of Atlantic hazel.

[1] http://www.snh.org.uk/strategy/saff.asp

sea scalewort (liverwort)

spring hazel cup (fungus)

frizzled pin-cushion (moss)

Peltigera collina
(lichen)

yellow specklebelly (lichen)

The biodiversity importance of Atlantic hazel

An example (above) of the diversity of species associated with Atlantic hazel at Ballachuan Hazelwood, SWT Reserve. This single leaning hazel by the path supported the **yellow specklebelly** *Pseudocyphellaria crocata* (the brownish-grey lobed lichen with dotted yellow powdery edges), and on the top of the branch the grey-lobed lichen *Peltigera collina*, both 'old woodland' species for which the UK has International Responsibility. The green moss is the **frizzled pin-cushion** *Ulota phyllantha*, and the brownish-red area near the top is the leafy liverwort **sea scalewort** *Frullania teneriffae*. The brown, scurfy cups are the fruiting bodies of the fungus **spring hazel cup** *Encoelia furfuracea*.

This small example demonstrates some of the special qualities of Atlantic hazel that make it a habitat of international importance. There is a concentration of diversity, a wealth of bryophytes, fungi and lichens. Some of these species are rare or endangered elsewhere in Europe, but can be found in wonderful profusion in the 'core' areas of the Atlantic hazelwoods.

Notable lichens associated with Atlantic hazelwoods, showing the strength of association, lichen community type and conservation status/priority.

Notable lichens associated with Atlantic hazelwoods	Star rating[2]	Graphidion[3]	Lobarion[4]	BAP[5]	Nr/Ns[6]	IR[7]
Arthonia cohabitans	***	Gr		BAP	Nr	IR
Arthonia excipienda	**	Gr			Nr	
Arthonia ilicinella	**	Gr			Nr	IR
Arthothelium dictyosporum	*	Gr		BAP	Nr	IR
Arthothelium macounii	***	Gr		BAP	Nr	IR
Arthothelium norvegicum	*	Gr			Nr	
Arthothelium orbilliferum	**	Gr			Ns	IR
Bactrospora homalotropa	**	Gr			Ns	IR
Collema fasciculare	**		L	BAP	Ns	IR
Eopyrenula septemseptata	***	Gr			Nr	IR
Fuscopannaria sampaiana	**		L	BAP	Ns	IR
Gomphillus calycioides	**		L	BAP	Ns	IR
Graphis alboscripta	***	Gr		BAP	Nr	IR
Lecanora cinereofusca	**	Gr		BAP	Nr	
Lecidea erythrophaea	*	Gr		BAP	Nr	
Leptogium brebissonii	**		L	BAP	Ns	IR
Leptogium cochleatum	**		L	BAP	Ns	IR
Leptogium hibernicum	**		L	BAP	Nr	IR
Melaspilea atroides	***	Gr			Ns	IR
Mycomicrothelia atlantica	**	Gr			Nr	
Parmeliella testacea	**		L	BAP	Ns	IR
Polychidium dendriscum	*		L	BAP	Nr	IR
Porina hibernica	*		L	BAP	Ns	IR
Pseudocyphellaria intricata	**		L	BAP	Ns	IR
Pseudocyphellaria norvegica	**		L	BAP	Ns	IR
Pyrenula coryli	***	Gr			Nr	
Pyrenula hibernica	***	Gr		BAP	Nr	IR
Pyrenula laevigata	**	Gr			Ns	IR
Sticta canariensis	*		L	BAP	Nr	IR
Thelotrema macrosporum	***	Gr			Ns	IR

2   Degree of strength of association with Atlantic hazelwoods, with *** being exclusively associated, ** closely associated, * mildly associated

3   *Graphidion*: indication that the species occurs in the *Graphidion* community (mostly on smooth bark)

4   *Lobarion*: indication that the species occurs in the *Lobarion* community (mostly on rough bark)

5   BAP = Biodiversity Action Plan species

6   Nr/Ns = Nationally rare/Nationally scarce

7   IR = species for which the UK (more particularly, Scotland) has International Responsibility (Woods & Coppins 2003)

What is the global importance of Scotland's Atlantic hazel?

Hazel is fairly common along the Atlantic seaboard in western Scotland, particularly from Knapdale and Arran in the south, to southern Sutherland in the north, often seen as small fragments or patches at the edges of other woodlands, or along roadsides, but occasionally as quite significant stands. The biodiversity value of these hazel habitats can be quite varied. The 'core' hazelwoods provide a unique habitat of high biodiversity value, with species and communities of bryophytes, fungi and lichens that are of international importance. Hazelwoods currently of lower biodiversity value are nonetheless important in providing potential future habitat, allowing expansion and linkage between the present 'core' hazelwoods. The particular importance of the habitat is the result of a combination of climate, location (hence 'Atlantic'), and long-established history of a habitat that has had little – if any – major disturbance.

Some of the **Atlantic hazelwoods** found in western Scotland, western Ireland, more rarely in south-west England and Wales, and as fragments in the French Atlantic Pyrenees and in Norway, are believed to be relict stands of ancient woodland. They form a distinctive habitat that appears to be a unique feature within the **coastal temperate rainforests** of the world.

Coastal temperate rainforests – a global perspective

(WWF classified eco-regions of the world, subdivided into 17 priority 'Major Habitat Types (MHTs), to describe areas of the world that share similar environmental conditions, habitat structures, patterns of biological complexity, etc. (Rhind 2003). Within the broad category of temperate broadleaf and conifer forest habitat, coastal temperate rainforest was recognised as a distinctive biome. In global terms, coastal temperate rainforest is extremely rare, confined to just seven regions in the world: the Pacific Northwest; the Valdivian forests of south-western South America; New Zealand; Tasmania (and a strip along New South Wales of south-east Australia); the north-eastern Atlantic (including the Pyrenees, West Highlands of Scotland, Ireland, Norway and Iceland); south-western Japan, and the eastern Black Sea. The total world area of coastal temperate rainforests is estimated to be only 302,227km[2] (Rhind 2003).

This biome experiences **high rainfall**

Lobaria scrobiculata, a lichen for which the UK has International Responsibility, growing on an old hazel by Sonachan Hotel, Ardnamurchan, 2005.

John Douglass

(with over 1,500mm of annual rainfall), but some parts are effectively even wetter through having a **large number of 'wet days'** (a day with at least 1mm of precipitation). The regularity of 'wetting' throughout the year keeps some areas constantly damp and humid (Averis et al. 2004). Added to this is 'occult' precipitation, or sea-mists, which condense as water droplets on coastal vegetation. Temperatures are generally mild and do not vary greatly between summer and winter (**equable**). An **index of climatic oceanicity** has been calculated (Averis *et al.* 2004) which demonstrates that north-west Scotland and western Ireland have the most oceanic climate in Europe, and this is why these areas are of international importance for 'oceanic' bryophytes, lichens and ferns.

In north-western Scotland, this biome is estimated to amount to 6,895.8km[2], and broadly includes woodlands dominated by oak, birch and hazel, where trees and rocks are often thickly clothed with bryophytes, lichens, ferns and fungi, leading to these woods being termed the **Celtic rainforest**.

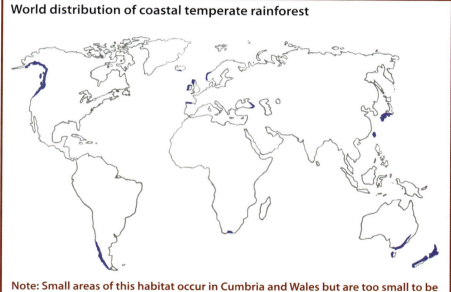

World distribution of coastal temperate rainforest

Note: Small areas of this habitat occur in Cumbria and Wales but are too small to be shown on this map; the 'cloud forests' in the Azores, Madeira and Canary Islands are also regarded as a type of coastal temperate rainforest. (Map from Averis *et al.* 2011)

❛The Atlantic hazelwoods are a crucially important component of this habitat, and are particularly important for lichens, bryophytes and fungi.❜

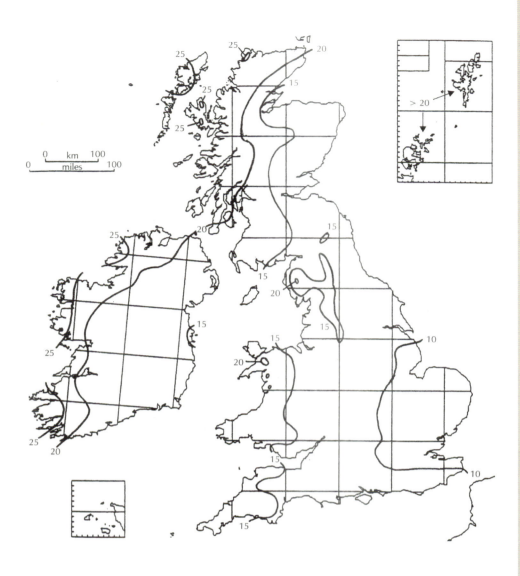

Pale-blue dots: pre-1960; dark-blue dots: post-1960; red dots: post-2000. (Maps generated from the Scottish Site Lichen Database, available on the NBN).

Arthonia ilicinella

Arthothelium macounii

Index of climatic oceanicity

This index is calculated as the mean annual number of wet days (> 1mm) (Ratcliffe 1968) divided by the range of monthly mean temperatures (°C) (Meteorological Office 1952). Higher values indicate a more oceanic (wetter and/or more equable) climate. Atlantic hazel occurs within areas having an index of 20 or more.
(Map from Averis *et al*. 2004).

Examples of lichens associated with Atlantic hazelwoods which clearly fall within 20+ index of oceanicity include the following *Graphidion* and *Lobarion* species:

(i) *Graphidion* species: **Arthonia ilicinella**, Red Data Book (RDB) category as Near Threatened, Nationally scarce (Ns), an apparent UK endemic species, and a species for which the UK has International Responsibility (IR);
Arthothelium macounii, RDB Vulnerable, Nationally rare (Nr), BAP species, IR;
Bactrospora homalotropa, Ns, IR;
Graphis alboscripta, RDB Near Threatened, a BAP species, a Scottish endemic species (therefore IR), Ns;
Melaspilea atroides, Ns, IR;
Thelotrema petractoides, IR. (Note: where records are shown further east, these usually refer to oceanic species found as relicts on hazel within ravines, where lack of disturbance and conditions are comparable with climatic conditions further west.)

(ii) *Lobarion* species: **Degelia atlantica** IR;
Pseudocyphellaria norvegica, BAP species, Ns and IR.

Bactrospora homalotropa

Graphis alboscripta

Melaspilea atroides

Thelotrema petractoides

Degelia atlantica

Pseudocyphellaria norvegica

Hazel dynamics

Old-growth Atlantic hazel, the 'core' stands

The special crustose lichens of the *Graphidion* (the 'script' lichens) and the foliose (leafy-lobed) lichens of the *Lobarion* found on Atlantic hazel are all considered species which require 'old-growth' woodland, or long periods of ecological continuity (Rose 1976, 1992; Coppins & Coppins 2002). **These lichens are not present in hazel that has been coppiced. Nor are they present in hazel stands that have recently expanded.** So, for example, the extensive hazel scrub found today on the Burren, in Co. Clare, Western Ireland, is largely species-poor,

with few examples of crustose *Graphidion* or the foliose *Lobarion*. Importantly, the Burren does, however, retain certain key pockets of richness – remnant core areas of high biodiversity, where the hazel gloves fungus can also be found, but there is nothing here approaching the richness of the western Scottish Atlantic hazelwoods. The same comments apply to the hazel on the limestone in Co. Fermanagh. Although, in a Northern Irish context, there are some important areas for lichens within the hazel, there is nothing that comes close to some of the Scottish woodlands.

So, how does Atlantic hazel maintain an old-growth habitat?

Hazel dynamics

A typical hazel has a cluster of thin, medium-sized and thick stems. The smooth-barked young stems are colonised by the crustose lichens of the *Graphidion*. As these stems become older and thicker, the bark roughens and crustose lichens give way to bryophytes and foliose lichens of the *Lobarion*. The ageing stems tend generally to lean outwards, probably from the weight of the canopy they support. This creates a gap in the overall canopy, which enables new young stems to grow up and fill the space. Winter storms can damage the canopy, breaking off twigs, and abrasion from stems rubbing together in windy weather allows fungal pathogens (such as the glue fungus *Hymenochaete corrugata*) to attack and gradually kill off individual stems. This all leads to a considerable turnover of stems within the hazel.

New stems (whips) appear to be produced from the base of the hazel every year, and this is a critical feature. Initiation of new stem production may be triggered by short periods in spring when light conditions are favourable. When existing stems are in full leaf, forming a closed canopy, new stems will abort by late summer because of heavy shade. If a gap persists, however, then new spring whips are able to grow rapidly and fill the space. The annual production of new stems seems to act as a fail-safe strategy to ensure the continued viability of the hazel.

> In the right conditions, each hazel is a self-perpetuating ecological unit, always with some young, smooth-barked stems (supporting crustose lichens) and generally some older stems (supporting the foliose lichens). There is an unbroken cycle of replenishment, which is crucial for the ecological continuity required by the more specialised and niche-demanding old-woodland lichens.

Glen Nant, May 2010.

Ballachuan Hazelwood, 2010.

However, the plot thickens, since hazels in different situations tend to behave in slightly different ways – and the presence of grazing animals will further influence development of the hazel shrub.

Vigorous hazels in cattle-grazed pasture, Co. Fermanagh, 2010.

Peter Quelch

Examples of hazel layering: (top) at Achnatra, by Inveraray, Argyll, 2007, and (below) at Lochcarron, Wester Ross, 2007. In both instances, the hazels are in fairly disturbed open woodland, with low grazing impact.

On deep soils in sheltered conditions …

… the hazels tend to be large, well grown and widely spaced, with the canopies of adjacent hazels often meeting. In these situations, canopy spread can reach 6.5m in diameter, and canopy height can be more than 6m. These hazels tend to support mostly shade-tolerant old-woodland lichens of the *Lobarion*, with the more light-demanding species of the *Graphidion* only poorly represented. There are large numbers of stems per hazel, ranging from thin and spindly to very thick and woody, the latter becoming almost horizontal.

The canopy twigs of these collapsing stems gradually adjust to vertical as the main stem assumes a horizontal position. Hence, when the old stems eventually collapse, the canopy twigs are often well above browsing height. In some cases, layering of collapsed stems takes place and new hazel shrubs can be formed, but this is successful only if there is a space, as competition for light is a prime factor controlling successful hazel establishment. Within a closed canopy stand of hazel, the shade created by summer canopies in full leaf is extremely dark, which perhaps partly explains why tree seedlings are unable to establish and are rarely encountered.

On thin soils in exposed situations …

… shrubs tend to be closer together, with few thick woody stems. In these situations, *Lobarion* is often poorly represented, with *Graphidion* dominant on the smooth-barked young stems. There is a rigidity within the stand, with a tight, interlaced network of small twigs, which means that internally, the stand is very sheltered, although the outer twigs are often wind-clipped and distorted. Turnover of stems appears to be far more frequent, with the oldest stems often being no more than 12-15 years old (as a very rough rule of thumb, 1cm girth approximates to one year of growth). But despite appearances, hazels composed of young stems can be self-perpetuating old-woodland stands that may have persisted for thousands of years.

(Below) Hazelwood clothing a steep slope-face on the Isle of Luing, Argyll, 2010. The hazel canopy is tightly enmeshed together, and on fairly short stems, making this stand reasonably rigid and able to withstand Atlantic gales.

Ben Averis, 2009

Do individual hazels eventually die, or do they get progressively bigger?

Pollen evidence indicates that hazel arrived in western Scotland some 10,000 years ago, and persisted as a dominant shrub for something approaching 1,000 years (Birks 1989). Hazel has two strategies for reproduction:

- Hazel reproduces sexually, by wind-pollinated catkins. It is monoecious, that is, male flowers and female flowers are separate but both are present on the same bush. However, hazel does not self-pollinate, so for fertilisation to occur pollen from a different bush is needed (Alireza *et al.* 2004). To self-pollinate would produce clones of the parent plant, whereas cross-fertilisation allows genetic diversity. Successful fertilisation results in the production of seeds encased in hard, woody nuts. Nuts are an evolutionary adaptation that requires a vector (mammal or bird) to distribute them. They also float, and so can be carried along waterways.

- Hazel can also reproduce by cloning, whereby new shoots arise from the underground base; the term 'self-coppicing' is sometimes used to describe this mechanism. This last method could be argued as not strictly 'reproduction', as the original shrub remains and persists. As described in the previous section (under 'Hazel dynamics'), the above-ground woody stems will live for 15-50 years, depending on conditions and situation, and are regularly replaced by new shoots, so that the life of the hazel can be prolonged.

How long an individual hazel will live, given ideal conditions, is not known, and several ideas have been explored. Oliver Rackham, who has made intensive studies of trees, woodlands and woodland history, says:

'Unlike most ash and maple stools, a hazel stool is usually underground. Neglected stools often have a "self-coppicing" mechanism; stems die after 30-50 years and are replaced by new shoots. It is thus very difficult to tell the age of a hazel. The stools often reach 6ft (1.8m) in diameter but rarely much more. By analogy with other species this would represent an age of at least 300 years. It is possible that they cease to grow beyond a certain size, and they may even get smaller by underground decay.' (Rackham 2003)

Basal regeneration appears to occur each spring, with shoots arising from the outer edges of the hazel. If successful, these shoots will expand upwards until they reach canopy height, and then put out leaves. If these basal shoots are regularly browsed, then regeneration can also occur above browsing height by shoots springing from existing stems. However, in the absence of browsing, basal shoots will be regularly produced from the outer perimeter. Over time, this will lead to an increase in circumference of the hazel shrub until, over hundreds of years, it could be enormous. However, no hazels have been encountered with a gigantic basal circumference.

Based on casual observations from many western Scottish hazelwoods over several decades, some observers began to see what they interpreted as '**hazel rings**', rather like the fairy rings formed by fungi in old meadows. There appear to be a series of discrete hazels ('satellite stools'), seemingly arranged around an open space. Examples have been seen from Ballachuan and from Mull, where satellite stools were reported around an empty circular space measuring 1.1m-2.3m in diameter (Coppins & Coppins 2000a,c).

The hypothesis was formed that these satellite hazels may have evolved through a gradual outward expansion of new stems at the edge of a 'mother' hazel, until a point is reached whereby either the centre becomes too shaded, and central stems are unable to replenish this space owing to canopy shade from the outer, more vigorous stems, or the central rootstock may become aged and exhausted. The outer edges of the hazel retain vitality, and support the 'daughters' of the original mother shrub. **If this were the case, then all the satellites would essentially be clones, with the same genetic make-up**.

This was quite an exciting discovery; the potential extrapolation of this method of vegetative reproduction has interesting implications, if taken to logical conclusions. We imagined that, on some sites where we believed hazel had been continually present since the end of the Ice Age, then potential hazel rings would overlap in complex mosaics. Whole series of rings could perhaps be plotted, many overlapping with adjacent rings, and the satellite hazels could themselves in turn eventually become 'mother' shrubs and form further rings. Dynamics would, to some extent, be governed by the availability of space within the stand into which hazels could expand. Genetically related groupings could perhaps be traced and plotted, which in turn could lead to conclusions about the ecological history and dynamics of the stand. But, how might one test or prove this theory, and where would sexual reproduction from seeded hazel fit in with this scenario? Not to mention the complications arising from mammals collecting hazelnuts and stashing them under existing hazels, where uneaten nuts could regenerate and spring up to form new shrubs.

Simon Gulliver, an MSc student at the Royal Botanic Garden, Edinburgh, in 2002, undertook the first exploratory investigation into the genetics of hazel from observed hazel rings (Gulliver 2002). He sampled six hazel rings and, on a broader scale, six transects at Ballachuan Hazelwood.

Ballachuan Hazelwood, 2010. A possible 'hazel ring', a group of hazels forming a circle around an open space. This could be the result of a coincidental way in which the individual hazels have arisen, or it may be because an ancient hazel has expanded outwards, and the middle part has subsequently decayed away.

Interior of Ballachuan Hazelwood, showing the spacing and structure of hazels in one part of the wood. Looking at the layout of the hazels, it is easy to 'imagine' potential rings. The work by Simon Gulliver, in 2002, was a first attempt to test the hypothesis of cloned daughter hazels forming rings. His samples were relatively small, but there were sufficiently positive results to provide a tantalising probability that the hazel ring idea has merit, and would benefit from further, more detailed investigation.

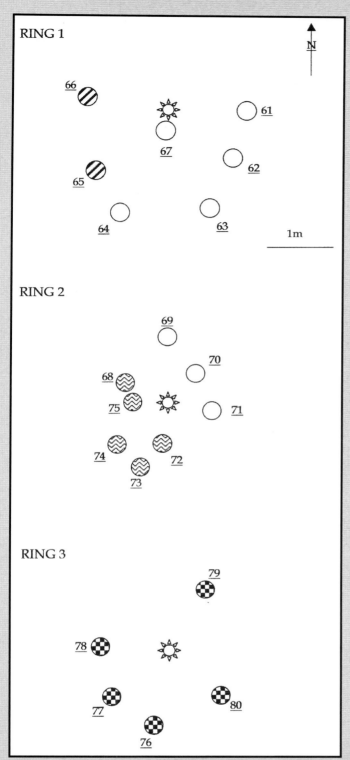

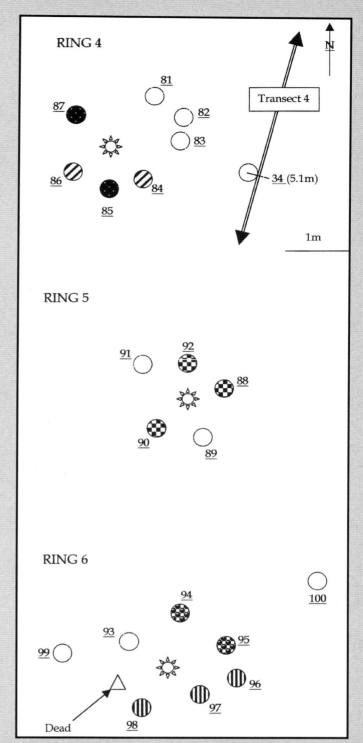

KEY:

Open circles: non-clonal stools
Shaded circles: stools identified as clonal
Stool number underlined (eg.1)
Notional centre indicated by star. Distances from the centre are to scale but not quantified in the figure. Stool size not to scale.

(Figure 3.2a) The results from sampling three observed hazel rings at Ballachuan Hazelwood. In this instance, only one proved unequivocally to be an entirely clonal ring (i.e. in Ring 3, where the diameter of the ring is 2.1m, the five individual satellite stools shared the same genotype). However, the findings also showed there was evidence that adjacent, but separate, individual hazels also shares clonality (e.g. Rings 1 and 2). (From Gulliver 2002)

(Figure 3.2b) Gulliver's (2002) results from rings 4-6. Most of the clonal companions seemed to occur only on one side of the ring, and two of the rings contained clones of two separate genotypes. It may be that on-the-ground perception of what constitutes a 'ring' is not correct. It may be that hazel expansion is not always concentric, but may be governed by other factors, such as availability of space from neighbouring hazels, etc. Gulliver's overall conclusion was that expansion of hazels is at a fine scale, rather than spreading widely throughout the site. As the pattern of clonality is thought to be linked to senescence of the central rootstock, Gulliver inferred that this 'disintegrator' pattern of clonal growth appears to promote long-term occupancy of existing territory, both at ground level and in the canopy. Six rings is a very small sample, but the evidence produced from this pioneering exercise is intriguing and certainly provides stimulus for further work. (From Gulliver 2002)

Dr Joe Hope Studying hazel at Loch a'Mhuilinn, West Sutherland, 2004.

How to age a hazel

Gulliver (2002) also reviewed the methodology used by a Finnish ecologist (Hæggeström 2000) to attempt to put an age on individual hazels. Hæggeström used two methods:

(i) correlating growth of hazel stands on raised beaches in the Åland Islands to known dates of land uplift in the Baltic sea;

(ii) by applying a growth index, calculated by dividing the girth of hazel stems by their age, then using the mean growth index (0.87) to calculate the age of hazels against the circumference of the base.

Hæggeström arrived at an amazing age of 990 years for his oldest hazel. However, he found that, using the growth index, some appeared to be older than the calculated date of the locality. He discussed possible sources of error. These include variation in ring width (girth/age) between hazels according to situation, and the assumption that there is a direct correlation between girth increments of aerial stems and the underground base. An additional factor was that most of the hazels in his study area had a long history of coppicing in the 19th and early 20th centuries, with the unknown effect that coppicing would have had on the size and natural dynamics of the coppice stools.

Incidentally, Hæggeström (2000) had also noted the tendency of hazel to form open rings, a growth-form termed runna in the Swedish vernacular.

Gulliver (2002) applied Hæggeström's formula for estimating the age of two hazels at Ballachuan:

(i) Hazel stool 8 (in one of the six transects)
(ii) one of the hazel rings, Ring 3, as it is essentially one 'stool'.

The results are shown opposite.

Estimated ages of two hazel stools at Ballachuan Hazelwood, using the diameter and circumference girth of the largest (Stool 8) in Transect 1, and the diameter and girth of the clonal ring (Ring 3). (Adapted from Gulliver 2002)

	Dia. (m)	Girth (cm)	Hæggeström formula estimate*		
			Low (0.39) (yr)	Mean (0.87) (yr)	High (1.60) (yr)
Stool 8	1.1	350	897	402	219
Ring 3	2.1	660	1692	759	412

* Based on annual stem growth (using lowest, mean and highest values from 84 hazels studied).

Clearly, further investigation into alternative methods for attempting to estimate the age of hazels needs to be carried out, and it is unlikely that one simple, foolproof method will ever be widely applicable. Nevertheless, even if the youngest estimates for the age of the two hazels at Ballachuan are accepted, it puts a whole new perspective on the way we should perhaps consider the ecological importance of Atlantic hazelwoods, as potentially one of the longest surviving, relict habitats in Scotland.

Ballachuan Hazelwood, 2010.

Flowers, ferns, bryophytes, fungi and lichens

The flowering plants, grasses and ferns of Atlantic hazelwoods

By Ben Averis

In western Scottish hazel-dominated woodland, the ground vegetation is varied. The commonest type is a mixture of grasses, flowering plants and bryophytes that belongs to the oak-birch-wood sorrel woodland, with hard-fern sub-community (NVC type W11b).

In many places, especially on limestone, the ground vegetation is less grassy and more dominated by flowering plants, and these hazelwoods are the extreme north-western representation of the broader ash–rowan–dog's mercury woodland (NVC community W9), which can develop in exposed situations in the windy far north-west of the British Isles. Hazel-dominated woodland can occupy a wide range of soil types, ranging from basic to mildly acid.

Despite exposure in some places, the climate here tends to be moderate, and this, combined with the extreme humidity, helps give the woodland its markedly oceanic character, with an abundance of bryophytes, lichens and often ferns. The pronounced wetness of the climate also means that the soils are typically permanently moist.

Wood anemone making a wonderful show in early spring, Argyll, 2006. Fronds of hard-fern can be seen on the right, and two small flowers of wood sorrel are present.

The irregular topography characteristic of this coastal zone influences the vegetation, with plants forming complex mosaics over the highly uneven, often steep and sometimes unstable soils, boulder scree and upland ravines. Often, local flushing adds further variety. **Dog's mercury** *Mercurialis perennis*, and **bluebell** *Hyacinthoides non-scripta* can be common in these woods in spring and early summer. Other species which are found include **enchanter's-nightshade** *Circaea intermedia*, **wood-sorrel** *Oxalis acetosella*, **wood anemone** *Anemone nemorosa*, **wood avens** *Geum urbanum*, **false brome** *Brachypodium sylvaticum*, **primrose** *Primula vulgaris*, **tufted hair-grass** *Deschampsia cespitosa* and **common dog-violet** *Viola riviniana*. Species such as **melancholy thistle** *Cirsium helenioides* and **globe flower** *Trollius europaeus* give a distinctly 'northern' feel. Ferns are often present: **male-fern** *Dryopteris filix-mas*, **lady-fern** *Athyrium filix-femina*, **bracken** *Pteridium aquilinum* and **hard-fern** *Blechnum spicant*, to name but a few. More localised lime-loving ferns which may also be found include regionally unusual plants such as **hart's-tongue** *Phyllitis scolopendrium* and **maidenhair spleenwort** *Asplenium trichomanes* or, at a higher altitude, the less common **green spleenwort** *A. viride*.

See **http://www.plant-identification.co.uk/skye/** for more details of these species.

Enchanter's-nightshade can tolerate fairly dense summer shade in the western hazelwoods.

Other characteristic spring flowers of western hazelwoods include primrose and dog-violets. Most of the ground flora of these hazelwoods is spring flowering, coming out before the leaves open on the hazel. Once the hazel canopy is in full leaf, the interior of the wood can be very dark.

The flowers, ferns, bryophytes, fungi and lichens of Atlantic hazelwoods　43

A fresh ferny edge creating a secret dell onto the bluebells
and grasses of the hazelwood at Barnluasgan, Argyll, May 2011.

Mary Gibby

Ben Averis

Two ferns characteristic of Atlantic hazel: hay-scented buckler-fern *Dryopteris aemula* (left and above), and below, the golden-scaled male-fern, *D. affinis*

Ben Averis

The bryophytes (mosses and liverworts) found in Atlantic hazelwoods

By Ben Averis, Gordon Rothero and Sandy Coppins

The deep greenness of the mosses and liverworts, clothing rocks, trunks and leaning branches, and climbing up the bases of hazels, provides the quintessential atmosphere of the 'Celtic rainforest'. Truly oceanic bryophytes require fairly constant levels of humidity in order to thrive, so generally are found in sheltered habitats and niches, away from bright sun or drying winds, and they are tolerant of low light levels. When entering a hazel stand, you become aware of its 'mossiness' only when you have penetrated a little distance into the stand, where the closed canopy forms a secure, sheltered and undisturbed habitat, ideal for the development of oceanic bryophytes.

David Genney

A damp, mossy hazelwood on Raasay, 2009.

Typically, the Atlantic hazelwoods boast a good diversity of oceanic bryophytes, with an abundance of the more common western species, but many very special oceanic species are also frequent. Perhaps the commonest moss on hazel in the western Highlands is **dwarf Neckera** *Neckera pumila*, but other common mosses include the **slender mouse-tail moss** *Isothecium myosuroides var. myosuroides*, **common feather-moss** *Kindbergia praelonga*, **common striated feather-moss** *Eurhynchium striatum*, **short-beaked wood-moss** *Loeskeobryum brevirostre* and the **neat feather-moss** *Pseudoscleropodium purum*. Oceanic (Atlantic) species typically include the **frizzled pincushion moss** *Ulota phyllantha* and the **lesser yoke-moss** *Zygodon conoideus*, as well as the liverworts **sea scalewort** *Frullania teneriffae*, **pointed pouncewort** *Harpalejeunea molleri*, **toothed pouncewort** *Drepanolejeunea hamatifolia*, **petty featherwort** *Plagiochila exigua* and **Killarney featherwort** *P. bifaria*. More notably, two scarce oceanic species – the **balding pincushion moss** *Ulota calvescens* and the **liverwort minute pouncewort** *Cololejeunea minutissima* – grow mainly on western hazels.

The striking leafy liverwort **sea scalewort** *Frullania teneriffae*, **here seen on rock, also commonly grows on hazel.**

The elegant dwarf Neckera *Neckera pumila*, on a horizontal hazel branch, Glen Nant, 2008.

Examples of the beautiful diversity of bryophytes associated with Atlantic hazel:

Top right: the shaggy-textured **Killarney featherwort** *Plagiochila bifaria*

Right: the delicate chains of the **toothed pouncewort** *Drepanolejeunea hamatifolia*

Above: the pale, feathery fronds of the **short-beaked wood-moss** *Loeskeobryum brevirostre*.

Fungi found in Atlantic hazel stands

By Liz Holden

Although there are many fungi that are recorded as growing in association with hazel, there are relatively few that are specific to hazel itself. Hazel is ectomycorrhizal, which means that it grows in a close (symbiotic) relationship with certain fungi: the fungi are intimately associated with the roots of the hazel and enable the tree to take up nutrients, which help to enhance its growth. In return, the fungus receives excess sugars from the hazel, enabling it also to thrive.

Fiery milkcap *Lactarius pyrogalus* is the most common mycorrhizal hazel associate. When damaged, this species exudes a fiery-tasting milky substance. Another large toadstool that is recorded with hazel in Scotland is the **hazel bolete** *Leccinum pseudoscabrum*, with tubes under the cap rather than gills, and flesh that blackens on exposure to air. Mycorrhizal fungi are often sparse in hazel woodland. It has been suggested that soils characteristic of hazel woodland (known as **mull humus**, resulting from plant remains being successfully broken down by small creatures in the soil, including plenty of earthworms) support fewer species and lower fruit-body production than mor soils (**mor soils** are associated with acidic conditions such as coniferous woodlands or acid moorlands, where cool, wet climatic conditions support fewer soil fauna, so the organic matter is not broken down so quickly).

Sometimes, you can be lucky in hazelwoods and discover some rarely reported fungi. At Morvern, **Atlantic bells** *Chromocyphella muscicola* has been recorded, the fruit bodies of which form delicate clusters of bell-shaped cups on the reddish-brown, leafy liverwort *Frullania*. Another unusual fungus is the striking **scarlet elf cup** *Sarcocypha austriaca*, a distinctive orange-red cup fungus, growing in the spring on fallen twigs and branches in leaf litter.

A fungus seen on a range of deciduous trees, but frequently on old hazels in woodlands is **Bleeding Broadleaf Crust** *Stereum rugosum* (seen right, overgrowing the **Green Satin lichen** *Lobaria virens*). This is a particularly young and fresh example of the fungus, which can exude blood-like droplets if scratched or bruised.

Many obvious fungi are saprotrophic – they break down and feed on dead plant or woody material, so are the great recyclers of the fungal world. Swarms of small dark bumps are visible throughout the year on dead wood, each about 3mm

Scarlet elf cup *Sarcocypha austriaca*, on fallen hazel twigs, Ballachuan Hazelwood, 2005.

Liz Holden

Bleeding Broadleaf Crust *Stereum rugosum*, Barnluasgan Hazelwood, Argyll, May 2011.

across. These are the fruit bodies of **hazel woodwart** *Hypoxylon fuscum*. **Spring hazel cup** *Encoelia furfuracea*, however, usually appears for a short time in the spring as brown, scurfy, cup-shaped fruit bodies, also on dead wood. A much rarer relative of this fungus is **green hazel cup** *E. glauca*, which favours these western woodlands. Even discarded nutshells of the hazel are decomposed by fungi, and the tiny, stalked disc fungus, **nut disco** *Hymenoscyphus fructigenus*, is worth searching for.

Winter storms will damage the canopy, breaking off twigs, and abrasion from stems rubbing together in windy weather allows fungal pathogens to get a hold and gradually kill off individual stems. This all leads to a considerable turnover of stems within the hazel. The fascinating **glue fungus** *Hymenochaete corrugata* has the ability (otherwise found mostly in the tropics), to 'glue' together and trap dead, fallen twigs that get lodged against living stems in the hazel, so preventing them from falling to the ground. This enables the fungus to feed on the dead wood, avoiding competition from other saprotrophs on the woodland floor. The glue fungus appears not to be present in all hazelwoods, but there is some indication that it is restricted to the less disturbed, old-growth hazel stands. So, if you notice the glue fungus sticking twigs to stems within a hazel bush, you may be in one of the 'special' hazelwoods.

Although occurring far less frequently, it is thought that the radiating lobes of **hazel gloves** *Hypocreopsis rhododendri* are in some way closely associated with the glue fungus, and may even be parasitic on it. Hazel gloves is a conspicuous species, which resembles a lichen in that it forms thick, rubbery, orange rosettes, reminiscent of minute orange washing-up gloves, with fingers or radiating lobes that clasp around the hazel stems. The species is thought to be an indicator of old-growth hazel woodland, and its presence puts you firmly in an Atlantic hazelwood habitat.

The accumulation of dead wood, both standing and fallen, is vital for woodland fungal diversity. As with the lichens, it is likely that ecological continuity is important to allow species such as hazel gloves to persist. The high degree of humidity in these woodlands will also be an important factor in the establishment of many of the wood-rotting fungi. Given these requirements, management by coppicing would be detrimental to the fungal diversity in the Atlantic woodland habitat.

Spring hazel cup *Encoelia furfuracea*, 2005

Examples of the **glue fungus**

These are all illustrations of the glue fungus on hazel, trapping fallen dead branches before they reach the ground. There are probably several species of *Hymenochaete* represented here, the most remarkable perhaps being the 'invisible' one (bottom) where the fallen branch is firmly glued by no obvious agent.

left: David Genney. Right: Peter Quelch

Examples of Hazel gloves

Hazel gloves is a distinctive fungus, with hard rubbery lobes like the fingers of orange rubber gloves. It is not known exactly how long the stroma persist on hazel stems. The examples shown here are in excellent health, although some stroma can be quite heavily browsed by slugs. On the opposite page, the lower far right example is a particularly large patch, measuring 14cm diameter; and the lower picture shows the fungus in its senescent dried state, when it is more difficult to spot.

Hazel gloves is a Biodiversity Action Plan (BAP) species, and a useful indicator of what may potentially be an important Atlantic hazelwood of high biodiversity interest, and is something to look out for.

Hazel gloves *Hypocreopsis rhododendri*, its spooky fingers clasping a hazel branch, with the **glue fungus** *Hymenochaete corrugata* 'gluing' a dead branch (right), Ballachuan Hazelwood, 2010.

Hazel gloves, grasping a dead hazel stem, Ballachuan Hazelwood, 2010.

More examples of the **hazel gloves** fungus *Hypocreopsis rhododendri*.

David Genney.

Lichens found in Atlantic hazel

By Brian and Sandy Coppins

Young hazel stems have smooth bark, and when they grow rapidly, straight up to reach a gap in the canopy, they are the characteristic 'hazel' colour. These are known as 'sun-shoots'. Sometimes, the thin outer epidermal layer will split and fray, like a flimsy skin. When the top of the stem reaches the canopy gap and puts out leaves, growth-rate slows, and the smooth bark of young stems becomes firmer. In Atlantic hazel stands, this is when the smooth bark begins to be colonised by small lichens, which appear as coloured patches (crustose lichens) forming mosaics over the bark. Several of these small lichens are found only in Britain in the Atlantic hazelwoods, and some are not known anywhere else in the world. These 'special' lichens seem to be restricted to stands that have occupied the same sites for long periods, and where there has never been any major disturbance or intensive management, such as coppicing.

First bark colonisers – endophloeodal (under the skin) species

Some of the small lichens that are the earliest colonisers of smooth hazel bark are hardly lichens at all, but small commensalistic bark fungi, which appear to link in with green chlorophyll cells occurring in the outer, thin bark. These are termed 'non-lichenised' fungi, but are traditionally considered 'honorary' lichens and are studied and recorded with the lichens. Hence, species lists from Atlantic hazel will include species from genera such as *Arthopyrenia, Arthothelium, Eopyrenula, Tomasellia* etc.

Sometimes, these hardly discolour the host bark at all, and it is only the fruiting bodies that reveal their presence. These fruiting bodies occur as tiny blackish dots and dashes, covered with a very fine 'skin'. This skin is, in fact, the fine, outer epidermal layer of the hazel bark, so the fruiting bodies of these non-lichenised fungi are also referred to as endophloeodal species, i.e., they occur 'under the skin'. Other small crustose species are 'true' lichens, in that they are both a fungus and an alga combined, i.e. they have their 'own' algae, and do not use the chlorophyll in the bark cells of the hazel. These grow on the outer surface of the smooth bark, and some have small dark or pale dots, while others have lines, like scribbles. It is this last group (the 'script' lichens) that lend their name to this group, the *Graphidion*.

Arthothelium macounii. Magnified x5, on smooth hazel bark.

Melaspilea atroides (image x2).

Thelotrema petractoides (image x2).

One of the more Atlantic hazelwood rarities, *Pyrenula laevigata*, here in perfect condition, with a slight purplish hue to the fruiting bodies (image x5).

Arthonia cinnabarina on hazel, one of the more striking crustose lichens, with a bright chilli-red powdery surface to the fruiting bodies (image x5).

Examples of crustose lichens forming mosaics on the outside of smooth bark of hazel: (left) *Pyrenula macrospora*; (below) *Lecanora chlarotera, Lecidella elaeochroma, Pertusaria leioplaca*; (bottom of page) *Graphis alboscripta*, the **white script lichen**, known only from ancient hazel stands in western Scotland.

John Douglass

White script lichen *Graphis alboscripta*, a BAP species, nationally rare, Scottish endemic, Red Data Book listed as Near Threatened (image x2).

Neil Sanderson

Blackberries in custard *Pyrenula hibernica*, Red Data Book Vulnerable, nationally rare, a BAP species, and a species for which the UK has International Responsibility, and listed on Schedule 8 of the Wildlife and Countryside Act. This is another example of a very rare crustose lichen that is known only in the British Isles from Atlantic hazelwoods in undisturbed ravines or steeply wooded cliffs, in north-west Scotland, west Wales and south-west Ireland. Elsewhere in the world, found only in Macaronesia.

A young hazel stem completely encased in the crustose lichen *Pyrenula macrospora*. This lichen is fairly common in Atlantic hazelwoods. It forms a thick, waxy coat over the surface of the hazel bark. The small black dots are the fruiting bodies of the lichen, where spores are liberated out into the air within the woodland. The greyish lines are boundaries between individual lichens on the stem, which meet up and form closed mosaics. When it rains, the rainwater drains down over the smooth, waxy lichen, and the outer surface dries quickly.

The grey-brown leafy plant is another lichen, *Leptogium cochleatum*. This is a real oceanic specialist, needing damp, humid conditions. It is attached here, and will soak up rainwater collecting in the cruck of the hazel stem.

The chestnut-coloured discs are the fruiting bodies of this lichen. Can you spot the tiny, whorled wood snail sheltering just below this lichen?

Perhaps the most charismatic and best known of the leafy-lobed lichens found on Atlantic hazel (and generally in the moist Celtic woodlands of ash and oak) is the **tree lungwort** *Lobaria pulmonaria* (above), at Dundonnell, 2007. This lichen lends its name to the community of Atlantic, leafy-lobed lichens, the *Lobarion*. This community tends to occur on rougher hazel bark of older stems, often with bryophytes.

Here is a fine example (left), looking its best in spring sunshine after morning rain, Taynish NNR, 2005. The raised ridges on the upper surface are roughened with coarse granules (soredia). These become eroded and are carried off in the wind, or are sometimes picked up on birds' feet when they are searching for small insects hiding in the mosses and lichens. The soredia lodge in moss or bark, growing into young *Lobaria pulmonaria*.

yellow specklebelly

smooth loop lichen

tree lungwort

Old, leaning hazel stems supporting a wealth of lichens of the *Lobarion* community, Lochcarron, 2003: tree lungwort *Lobaria pulmonaria*, smooth loop lichen *Hypotrachyna laevigata*, yellow specklebelly *Pseudocyphellaria crocata* and plum-fruited felt lichen *Degelia plumbea*.

plum-fruited felt lichen

tree lungwort

John Douglass

A lovely old veteran hazel 'tree' in a wood-pasture habitat at Loch a'Mhuilinn SSSI, West Sutherland, 2004. The trunk may be over 100 years old. At the base, a few young regenerating stems (looking like thin, dry sticks) have been nibbled off by deer. The trunk is clothed in bryophytes and lichens, mostly the leafy-lobed **tree lungwort** *Lobaria pulmonaria*, forming a greeny-brown 'shawl' and extending up the trunk. The blue-grey patches are **lob scrob** *Lobaria scrobiculata* and the **mealy-rimmed shingle lichen** *Pannaria conoplea*. Bryophytes cover the background as green, reddish-brown and golden-green patches. At the base, the white patches are crustose lichens.

Below, **Octopus suckers** *Collema fasciculare*, Laggan, Mull, 2005, and left, **frilly-fruited jelly skin** *Leptogium burgessii*, Loch Etive, Argyll, 2005. Both are examples of jelly lichens that are very restricted to the damp Atlantic climate.

John Douglass

John Douglass

Atlantic hazel habitat management

Atlantic hazel habitat examples and management recommendations

Atlantic hazel is a remarkably durable and persistent shrub. Because Atlantic hazel occurs in so many different stand types – from 'pure' stands to components of other bits of scattered woodland, as linear strips beside tracks and roads, or as mosaics in glades, valleys or cliff-sides – and has persisted under various management regimes over the centuries, it can be seen in all sorts of guises. Attempting to categorise Atlantic hazel proves to be difficult. Because hazel is so adaptable to changing environments – from intensively grazed habitat to one where all grazing is excluded – the form that hazel assumes within these management extremes can be quite dramatic.

However, in order to present some sort of workable scenario to recognise, assess, evaluate and provide appropriate management advice, some attempt needs to be made to provide guidelines to categorise hazel in its various states. The following four categories are not foolproof, by any means; more often than not, an area of Atlantic hazel will contain more than one of the stand types described.

Loch a'Mhuilinn, 2004. Illustrating the problem of trying to categorise Atlantic hazel into simple stand types: This was a veteran hazel 'tree', with an old, typically leaning thick 'trunk', developed as a result of long-term intensive grazing (Type C). Subsequently, with removal of grazing, strong, viable basal growth has arisen, so the hazel is reverting to a multi-stemmed form. So, is this now Type B?

Examples, with management guidelines, for various stand types of Atlantic hazel

1. **Closed-canopy, multi-stemmed stands of pure hazel**   **Type A**

2. **Scattered hazels in pasture (a broad, catch-all category)**   **Type B**

3. **Antique, veteran hazels**   **Type C**

4. **Hazel in woodlands (including ravines)**   **Type D**

Ballachuan Hazelwood, SWT Reserve, Isle of Seil, Argyll, 2006: 23ha of hazel on an epidiorite ridge, a classic Type A stand.

1. Type A: Closed-canopy, multi-stemmed stands of pure hazel (i.e. >75% hazel in the stand)

This is the habitat most often associated with Atlantic hazel, supporting the greatest range of biodiversity of bryophytes, fungi and lichens, and includes the classic sites of Ballachuan Hazelwood, Scottish Wildlife Trust (SWT) Reserve, Isle of Seil, Argyll, (Grid ref. NM 76 14), and the slope hazelwoods on the Isle of Eigg (Grid ref. NM 49 88).

Ballachuan Hazelwood

This is perhaps the best known and most quoted example of the Atlantic hazelwoods. The wood occupies an epidiorite ridge that runs along the south-eastern side of the Isle of Seil. The ridge is almost completely covered in hazel (23ha), with some open grassy areas on the top. The structure of the hazel stand varies throughout the site, according to the underlying topography.

(i) on thin, mineral soils on steep rocky slopes: individual hazels tend to have few stems; the canopy is often not above 2m and the stems are mostly slender (i.e. there is a fairly rapid turnover of stems, with an approximate maximum age of stem of 12-20 years, yet these hazels are known to support rare crustose lichen communities (the *Graphidion*), owing to the longevity and permanency of the stand and habitat).

(ii) in areas where soils are deeper, damp and loamy: the individual hazels tend to be large, with many stems, and in a wide range of sizes/ages (i.e. a longer periodicity of stem turnover). The hazels here are fairly widely spaced, with canopies reaching >3m. In these stands, lichens of the *Lobarion* community tend to be more dominant.

(iii) variation and gradations between these two basic stand structures.

There is, therefore, a considerable range of habitats present even within the confines of this hazelwood. The site is sympathetically managed by SWT for the wildlife interests. Apart from lichens, Ballachuan is notable for a species-rich ground flora, breeding birds and butterflies.

Inside Ballachuan Hazelwood, September 2010: hazels fairly evenly spaced, but each with relatively few, mostly small stems, indicating a fairly quick turnover; the oldest stem in this picture is probably no more than 30 years old. But this conditions – always having stems of different ages present, maintaining continuity year on year – has resulted in a species-rich habitat of rich biodiversity. There are a few young stems (or 'sun-shoots'), but only a few are needed to replenish the hazel every few years. However, this is an ancient stand, a 'core' hazelwood. These stems have all arisen naturally, and are not the result of being coppiced. You could walk through these woods and select the stems you need, cut them out (the term is 'drawing'), and leave the rest for another time. That way, continuity of conditions is retained within the stand, and there is a continual supply of suitable stems for different purposes. In the past, domestic animals would also be free to use the woodland as seasonal sheltered grazing without the need to elaborately fence off areas that needed protecting for coppice regrowth.

This part, today, is grazed only occasionally by deer. Bryophytes and leafy-lobed lichens are present in this fairly shaded section of the wood, with crustose lichens showing as pale patches on the smooth bark.

Another example of a typical **Type A** stand of hazel, in a small valley near **Ardslignish, Ardnamurchan, Argyll**, April 2007. Note the young willow and birch at the lower edge, with the hazel beyond forming a dense, closed-canopy stand.

Biodiversity value of hazel at Ballachuan

- Ballachuan Hazelwood is a Grade 1 Site of International Importance for its lichen interest, primarily for supporting the best examples of the western oceanic *Graphidion* community (the very special Atlantic 'script' lichens, that occur as coloured, crusty patches on smooth hazel bark), as well as the complementary species-rich *Lobarion* lichen community (the large, leafy-lobed lichens typical of Atlantic Celtic rainforests). Several Biodiversity Action Plan (BAP) species are included in the lichen assemblages found at Ballachuan.

- The **hazel gloves** fungus *Hypocreopsis rhododendri* (BAP and SAF species) is present; in some years it is locally abundant.

Management of Atlantic hazel at Ballachuan

- Today SWT carries out sympathetic management of the hazelwood, so there is no coppicing and no underplanting of native trees.

- SWT liaises with a local grazier, and some areas are grazed by cattle under a woodland grazing management agreement. There is careful monitoring of the effects of grazing on the hazel, as well as the associated species-rich grasslands.

- Some areas are fenced against grazing by cattle, although deer do browse in these parts of the wood.

- The overall effect of this sympathetic management has been to maintain the integrity of the stand, with glades being kept open. In the grassy areas where cattle are fenced out, seedlings can establish, several making it on to become young hazel bushes within tall bracken. This seems to be a good management model.

View of the interior of **Ballachuan** (2000), a typical **Type A** hazel stand. Hazels forming a closed canopy here are on fairly deep soils, so individuals are well formed, with a large number of stems, including older ones (probably 30 years old), but a high number of younger stems provide continuity within each plant and the stand. A high-biodiversity stand.

Ballachuan Hazelwood is perhaps the 'classic' example of this type of habitat in western Scotland. Other examples include Struidh Wood on Eigg, and coastal hazel along the Drimnin to Killundine SSSI, Morvern. With sympathetic grazing management, there is no reason why these Atlantic hazel woodlands should not persist indefinitely. This contrasts with other sites where over-grazing has led to serious decline of the habitat and a breakdown of the important internal structure of the stand, and at the other extreme, where all grazing is totally excluded, resulting in densely shaded thickets, loss of glades and reduction in biodiversity.

Slope hazelwoods on the Isle of Eigg

In the north of Eigg, parts of the steeply sloping sides below the basalt plateau of Beinn Bhuidhe are covered with stands of closed-canopy hazelwood. In the north-west, extensive areas of hazel occur above the settlement of Cleadale, including some fairly inaccessible stands under the basalt scarp.

On the other side of the island, below the east-facing scarp above the sea, lies Struidh Wood. This is a large stand of thick Atlantic hazel scrub which clothes the steep slope above small coastal meadows which were formerly used as summer pasture for cows with the sheilings of Struidh. In both these sites, the slopes are precipitous and occasional severe landslips occur, tearing away and taking sections of the wood with the landslip. Internally, these woods are dense, the canopy twigs short, contorted and interlaced, giving the internal structure a rigidity. It is also quite dark in summer, when the leafy canopy is fully out. There is a strong possibility that these slope hazelwoods have been continuously present since hazel first arrived in this part of Scotland, at least 9,500 years ago.

Hazel occurs widely on Eigg. In the south part of the island, around Galmisdale and Kildonan, there are small patches of scrub adjacent to open fields, beside tracks and roads, in small valleys or as a component of more mixed woodland. The island of Eigg is owned and managed by the people of the island, although the Scottish Wildlife Trust offers advice on habitat and wildlife management. The island is agricultural, but of low intensity. The comments on management for Atlantic hazel on Eigg apply equally to all areas of hazel occurring on the island, and are based on a brief report on the lichens carried out in 2000 (Coppins & Coppins 2000b).

Biodiversity value of hazel on Eigg

The **hazel gloves** fungus *Hypocreopsis rhododendri* (BAP and SAF species) is present in various patches of hazel around Galmisdale, Kildonan and Cleadale;

The **white script lichen** *Graphis alboscripta* (BAP and Scottish endemic) occurs on hazel at Struidh Wood, Cleadale and also near Kildonan.

Management of Atlantic hazel on Eigg, including Struidh Wood

On Eigg, hazel is to be retained, not coppiced. The main value of hazel on Eigg today is to provide sheltered grazing, although few animals appear to enter or scramble about on the steeper hazelwoods. In 2000, the present grazing regime appeared to be in balance with maintaining healthy and viable stands of hazel. Grazing within the stands results in both shaded and gladed areas, together with some thick, old mossy stems, and small, smooth-barked young stems, creating a wide range of conditions and niches.

View of Struidh Wood, on the east-facing basalt slope on Eigg, looking down onto the small coastal meadows and former sheilings.

The structure of the hazelwood is very similar to that above Cleadale, with a dense closed canopy. There is a continual replenishment of stems, creating a habitat that is structurally rigid and also gives continuous cover. These hazelwoods are known to support notable lichen communities, especially rare members of the *Graphidion*.

View of the thick, closed-canopy hazelwood on the basalt slopes above **Cleadale**, Isle of Eigg, 2010.

Problems and dilemmas with managing Atlantic hazel

The reason for concentrated pressure at this location is that a permanent feeding station is present, so cattle congregate in this area. Taken overall, biodiversity interest at present is medium; in some parts of the stand there is a good representation of the *Lobarion* and the hazel gloves fungus. The smooth-bark *Graphidion* are moderately well represented, although none of the more demanding, Atlantic 'special' species are present because the internal structure of the stand is breaking down. Clearly, this area of woodland is undergoing structural change, and the hazels will continue to deteriorate if there is no moderation of grazing pressure.

With continued grazing the canopy will continue to open up. Some hazels will be lost, whilst others will eventually adapt to a tree-like form, and a few may eventually develop into veteran hazels. Biodiversity interest would continue to decline as conditions within the stand change.

If grazing were removed there would be a flush of regeneration springing up from the base of the hazels. This would ultimately benefit the bryophytes, fungi and the *Lobarion*, but the 'special' small crustose lichens of the *Graphidion* would be lost to the site, with only common, widespread species colonising the smooth bark of the young stems.

The dilemma is how to accommodate the needs of the grazier, providing sheltered grazing for his stock over winter, yet at the same time ensuring that the habitat is not compromised past the point of rescue.

David Genney

Type A stand on its way to becoming **Type B** (scattered hazels in pasture). At present, this stand (top) conforms to a multi-stemmed, closed canopy (Type A), but this hazel stand is used extensively by young cattle as sheltered winter grazing. Hence, there is much evidence of trampling of the ground flora, stems are broken, basal regeneration is grazed, and in some areas, the hazels are beginning to be reduced to a few, thickened stems, with much evidence of browsing off of basal shoots (middle and bottom).

Luing, July 2010. Sheep and Luing cattle grazing on pasture between open-access wooded slopes, with mostly stands of dense hazelwood on the scarp slopes.

Luing, July 2010. In some areas – where sheep and cattle regularly gather – the impact of concentrated browsing, trampling and rubbing has reduced individual shrubs. This is a very localised effect, but is a good illustration of the possible long-term effects on continually, heavily overgrazed hazelwoods. Carl Farmer here, examining lichens.

Luing, July 2010. An example of a now-isolated hazel, reduced and damaged by sheep and cattle. The hazel still retains a healthy canopy, but on a reduced number of stems. Evidence of several recently broken stems can be seen, with the dead wood lying around. Sheep and cattle have free range over most of the island, and the numbers are relatively low, so this sort of impact is not seen elsewhere on the island, where closed-canopy stands of hazel are frequent

Luing, July 2010. Eventually, individual hazels are reduced by constant browsing, trampling and rubbing, and succumb. Here, remains of stumps can be seen in the grass. The tenacity of hazel is such that the rootstock remains viable for some time after 'death', and will continue to put up hopeful shoots, but these would inevitably be browsed at this locality.

Below: **Luing**, July 2010. Most hazel on Luing is unenclosed and of the closed-canopy Type A stand structure. There is good basal regeneration here, and little evidence of excessive browsing, trampling or breaking off of branches and stems. The current grazing management at Luing appears to be sustainable for the Atlantic hazel interest

Treshnish, Mull, May 2010. Formerly heavily grazed hazel now showing good recovery after the erection of a deer fence.

Treshnish, Mull, May 2010. Interior of the stand, showing how the hazels were often reduced to one or two stems before grazing was excluded, and basal regeneration is now successfully getting away. There is a good recovery of the ground flora, too.

photos above and left: Anand Prasad

Atlantic hazel habitat management **67**

2. Type B: Scattered and veteran hazels in pasture

This is probably the most usual way to find hazel throughout western Scotland. Sometimes, there are just a few relic hazel shrubs remaining in heavily grazed open pasture between patches of mixed woodlands. These scattered hazel shrubs rarely form a recognisable stand, although occasionally there are clumps of several together. The common feature of the hazels is the effect of long-term grazing on its shape and structure.

Biodiversity value – landscape and cultural value

The biodiversity value of these hazels tends to be rather low (the Durnamuck examples are too wind-blasted and exposed, for example), but occasionally a few lichens of the *Lobarion* community will persist on the damp, thickened stems. The cultural and landscape significance, however, is high, as these old hazels are relics of a bygone age, and are also clues as to past cultural practices. These hazels at Durnamuck, for example, sit atop a small ridge that has the fallen remains of an old dyke, plus what might be ruins of a dwelling or animal enclosure. It is not uncommon to find large hazels associated with field boundaries and isolated dwellings. Although it is unlikely that whole stools were completely cut over (coppiced in the English tradition), hazel was extensively used and valued. Individual stems would be selected and cut, the size of the stem cut varying according to purpose. By selecting stems, the base remained viable and did not have to be constantly guarded from browsing flocks and herds. It also meant that in favourable years when nuts were produced, there were sufficient stems to provide a good nut harvest, just outside the backdoor.

These examples (above) are growing in an open situation, and are subjected to regular browsing of basal shoots. The hazel has responded by producing strong, vigorous stems sufficient to bear the canopy at an elevated position. Each of these stems is almost like a small trunk. Growing on a slope, and with sheep often 'lying-up' under the shelter of the hazel so that hollows become excavated beneath, they can become unstable and vulnerable to wind-blow, and may eventually topple over. However, sufficient canopy is usually left projecting above browsing height in order for the hazel to survive and adapt yet again to new conditions. Durnamuck, Dundonnell, W Ross, 2007.

Further examples of scattered hazels in pasture

Glen Shira, by Inveraray, Argyll, 1996. An example of a hazel 'walking down' a slope. Under constant grazing, hazel is reduced to a single tree-like trunk, with the canopy held aloft. Being on a slope, the trunk becomes unstable and collapses down-slope (the arrow indicates the real base of this hazel). Some of the elevated canopy must have remained out of reach of browsing, and slowly adjusted to grow vertically, putting on strong growth. Layering does eventually occur at points where the stems lie close to the ground. At the base of the original shrub, regeneration shoots are still put up each year, but are always browsed off.

Scattered hazels in pasture is a broad category of a stand type, but this example is of scattered hazel in wood pasture, at Taynish, Argyll. These edge of woodland hazels border on to an open, brackeny slope, and provide a habitat that supports a wide range of wildlife, including birds, mammals and invertebrates, as well as flowering plants, fungi, lichens and bryophytes. The grazing in Taynish National Nature Reserve is minimal, apart from a few deer.

Peter Quelch

These examples of hazel in pasture are from Erray, Mull, 2000. On this site, there is a fairly well defined area of closed-canopy slope hazelwood which grades out (above and right) to scattered hazels in pasture. Grazing by sheep is moderate to high, and perhaps all year round. The scene above shows a discrete clump of hazel reduced to a few stems per shrub. These stems have thickened in response to any basal regeneration being continually thwarted by browsing. Right: This hazel 'tree' is also at Erray, and is the ultimate response to continual grazing – note the cluster of browsed regeneration at the base. The hazel here appears robust and secure, with the canopy held aloft, well above browsing height.

The biodiversity value is low to moderate. A period of reduction (or relaxation) from grazing would benefit the habitat.

Above: Perhaps an extreme example of hazel in permanently heavily grazed pasture, where every hazel is reduced to single stemmed 'trees'. Below: What happens when grazing is totally removed for an extended period – extensive regeneration from the base, plus surrounding thicket development. The introduction of conservation grazing is recommended.

Photos: Anna Griffith

Management of scattered hazels in pasture

Ensuring the retention of old hazels is important for wood-pasture habitat, landscape, cultural and aesthetic considerations, as well as recognition that the original hazels may be several centuries old, and have their own intrinsic value. If the hazel becomes unstable, or has toppled over, then remedial action can be carried out by putting up some temporary fencing, such as a few fence posts with rylock fencing, to keep browsing animals at bay. This needs to remain in place for as little as five years in order for the hazel to send up viable shoots.

Pre-emptive cutting of some potentially top-heavy stems may be an option. This has not been tried, but should be successful, something akin to pollarding, done above browsing height, so that new shoots would sprout from around the cut end.

Neil Sanderson

These enormous, veteran hazels from Geltsdale, Cumbria, bear witness to being part of a long-term pasture woodland, with widely spaced hazels and thickened stems that are as big as tree trunks. Browsing has been reduced, and a strong flush of new stems is well established. Such huge specimens would have been greatly valued for sheltered grazing, providing poles and stems for many uses and potential nut harvests. Management would be similar to that outlined above.

Ben Averis

3. Type C: Veteran hazels

The old hazel pictured above, is a survivor; it has managed to maintain a presence here when other hazels have seemingly succumbed to constant grazing pressure. It has deviated from its normal multi-stemmed form as a result of continual browsing of the basal shoots. The surviving 'stem' (or trunk) has gradually thickened over the years and the canopy proliferated above grazing height, forming a classic 'hazel tree'.

What is interesting about this example is that there appears to be a 'bolling' (a swelling at the top of the trunk). Bollings are characteristic features of pollarded trees (usually oak or ash), and are formed as a result of repeated pollarding, or cutting away of fresh branches from above browsing height. So, was this hazel 'tree' pollarded?

There are two opinions on this. There is no doubt that this looks like a classic example of a pollarded hazel. And there is no reason why hazel would not have been pollarded. On the other hand, there are also numerous examples of old hazels like this, where old extensions of the 'trunk' break away because of the strain and weight of the canopy, leaving a stump end which sometimes heals over and will appear as a rounded swelling. New stems will always be put up to maintain the canopy, thus giving the appearance of a 'pollard' growth form. It would be interesting to date the canopy branches (by coring). If they were less than 50 years old it would tend to discount pollarding – although it would be useful to tap into memories and recollections of local people, as to whether they remember this practice being carried out locally.

An example of a veteran hazel 'tree' amidst bouldery wood pasture (sheep in the background attest to grazing still being present), Stonethwaite, Cumbria, 2007

Richard Thompson

Rassal Ashwood NNR, 2004. In this example of a veteran hazel, it has been subjected to fairly intensive browsing over a long period, and has been reduced to a single thick and leaning 'trunk', supporting a canopy above browsing height. Part of the 'trunk' has rotted away (left), possibly broken off during a storm by the weight of the extended canopy. When browsing was removed, the basal shoots were able to get away, giving this ancient hazel a new lease of life, with a greatly expanded canopy. The old, gnarled stems were probably on the verge of dying off, but their decay is speeded up now that there are new stems to give life to the base of the hazel. Note also how hazel seedlings have established (bottom left) amongst the limestone rocks.

Ancient hazel at Rassal Ashwood, winter 2005

Another example of a flush of basal regeneration that has rejuvenated the ancient hazel above, at Rassal Ashwood, (http://www.snh.org.uk/publications/on-line/designatedareas/nnrs/RassalAshwood/RassalAshwood.asp). This shrub has not been coppiced or pollarded, but has developed this shape as a result of long periods of continual browsing. It has obviously toppled over at some time in the past, under the weight of the extended canopy, but sufficient of the canopy was able to persist out of reach of browsing animals. This developed into these old, leaning tree-like stems, which are now covered in bryophytes and leafy-lobed lichens of the *Lobarion*.

● **What would be the future for this hazel if browsing was not reduced?** It would most probably result in the eventual collapse of the old stems, and ultimately death. There has been very little tree-coring to age old hazel stems; dating has been rather *ad hoc*, counting rings where old hazels have fallen and been sawn up. We do not know how long an individual hazel stem can live. As a very rough rule-of-thumb guide, the girth of hazel stems in centimetres corresponds to the age of the stem. This is not so applicable to old, thick stems, however, as growth rate reduces with age, so girths of large stems such as those seen here could measure 70-80cm, and probably corresponds to more than 100 years in age.

● **What is the future of the hazel now that browsing has been stopped?** The base has certainly rejuvenated and gained a new lease of life. It is quite likely that the old trunk-like stems will decay, and this hazel will assume its multi-stemmed form, with new stems replacing older stems in the usual manner. Hence, in another ten years, this hazel will appear simply as a multi-stemmed shrub, and no doubt be casually regarded as perhaps having recently arisen amongst other 'new' hazels that are occurring here. And it may even be seen as a healthy example of hazel-coppice, with nothing to indicate its amazing past history and antiquity.

● **Will old, thick, woody stems develop as part of the rejuvenated hazel through natural dynamics, providing opportunities for bryophytes and leafy-lobed lichens to be present?** This is difficult to tell, as it will depend on whether grazing is reintroduced, and if so, at what level. With all grazing excluded, then it would be anticipated that the site would soon close over with thicket development of hazel (plenty of hazel seedlings are present already). In which case, the stem turnover could be fairly regular.

As Rassal is moderately sheltered and lies on limestone, it is noticeable that the canopies of hazels are quite high (see photograph on page 70), often reaching 6m, and this is in an open situation where the canopies are not being drawn up by competition from nearby tall trees. Consequently, growth rate is robust, and if the site became completely closed-in with regeneration, with no glades allowing light to filter between the shrubs, then it is likely that in low light levels, species-poor assemblages of bryophytes would begin to dominate older stems, rocks and ground in between. Rassal is recognised as being an example of wood pasture and is known to contain a herb-rich ground flora; this has been compromised in the past by intensive grazing, but could equally be compromised by lack of grazing.

Management of antique hazels is something of a dilemma

Option 1

Remove all grazing and allow the ancient base to send up masses of viable regeneration, so ensuring the long-term viability of the hazel. The old, trunk-like stems would eventually decay and perish. The hazel would still retain its 'ancient' status through the original rootstock, but would lose a feature characteristic of past site-management history, together with the epiphytes and invertebrates associated with the old, craggy veteran hazel trunks. Once established (say, five years), grazing can be reintroduced and the hazel will begin to function according to the levels of grazing, i.e. heavy and continuous grazing will lead eventually to the creation of another hazel, dominated by a few large, craggy stems (over maybe 50-70 years); with low to moderate grazing, the hazel will retain its multi-stemmed form, and persist indefinitely.

Option 2

Remove all grazing and allow the ancient base to send up masses of viable regeneration, so ensuring its long-term viability. After it is well established (say, five years), cut back a good proportion of the new regeneration, leaving perhaps five or six good stems to continue to produce a canopy, but not allowing these to compromise the function of the older stems. Reintroduce grazing, so that any new shoots sent up from the base of the hazel may be browsed off, whilst it still retains a viable canopy from existing, established regeneration. This option is purely theoretical and has not been tried, but attempts to ensure the perpetuation of the old feature of the hazel, yet ensure its long-term viability. It may be that the presence of even a few younger stems arising from the base of the stool will lead to decline of the older stems. But no tree-trunk can live forever and these old stems would eventually die, and without opportunity for regeneration to establish, the whole specimen would be lost.

It may be worth noting that the biodiversity value of hazel with old, craggy stems is similar to that of any veteran tree, i.e. craggy bark with niches associated with water retention and stem flow or water-seepage zones, plus areas of 'dry' bark, which rarely receive direct wetting, and are often shaded. There will also probably be areas of dead wood, again providing another niche of opportunity. So a range of epiphytes can be present which are adapted to the niches associated with veteran trees.

However, part of the biodiversity importance of Atlantic hazel lies in the epiphytes associated with the smooth bark of young stems. In hazels where there is a regular turnover of stems so that the multi-stemmed form is continuous, crustose lichens are plentiful, forming closed mosaics, and with the high possibility that the assemblage contains the 'specialist' species of the *Graphidion* lichen community which are found only in the Atlantic hazelwoods. In hazels that have assumed 'tree-like' growth forms, with veteran craggy stems and a high, thin canopy, the *Graphidion* community is poorly represented. There will have been a loss of the continuity of conditions within the tree, with no recruitment of new stems with smooth bark for crustose lichens to colonise when existing stems either die, or gradually get thicker, with rougher bark. The extended canopy, high up above browsing height, is too open and exposed to allow the full development of the *Graphidion* community. Hence, when grazing is removed and a flush of new stems does arise, forming a characteristic multi-stemmed hazel, these stems are invariably almost devoid of lichens, with only a few of the more common *Graphidion* species present. The loss of that intimate niche associated within long-term, multi-stemmed Atlantic hazels stands has led to a loss of the lichens that are dependent upon it. As these species are known to be poor colonisers with very limited dispersal ranges, it is unlikely that they will ever return.

Therefore, it is important to recognise and protect the stands of multi-stemmed Atlantic hazel that still persist.

The same hazel at Rassal as in the previous picture, but here showing the height of the canopy of the recent basal regeneration (See dog for scale). Note the typical 'gondola' shape to the shrub, created when the top-heavy old 'trunk' fell over, and thick, older stems above browsing height remained viable. Now, there are broken tops on the older stems, but they still support a significant, if somewhat thin, but viable canopy (2005).

Further examples of Type C veteran hazels

A strangely contorted veteran hazel with a very chequered history of survival, Dundonnell, Wester Ross, 2007. Despite permanent sheep grazing, this appears viable, with strong growth from a few well-established stems. Whether lopping the thick horizontal stem would benefit the shrub is debateable; bits have died away, presumably as new growth became established. How old is this hazel?

Hazels growing well on a sheltered south-east-facing wooded slope on Skye, at Leitir Fura, 2007. Hazels grow well on the base-rich soils, but have endured long periods of heavy browsing, which has reduced them from multi-stemmed to 'tree-like' form. Invariably, the extended canopy causes the old stems to collapse. Grazing has been removed (apart from deer), and there is now a resultant flush of even-aged regeneration of hazel, mostly arising from the base. Note that although the horizontal old 'trunk' is mossy, there are few, if any, lichens, although there is a rudimentary mottling of crustose lichens on the smooth stems.

Examples of 'antique' hazels on a slope above the Dundonnell River, Wester Ross, 2007. A classic collapse of the thick, old trunk with survival by regeneration above browsing height. This site is still quite heavily sheep grazed, so basal regeneration is still browsed off. Smooth bark has negligible lichen cover.

Old pasture woodland at Leitir Fura, on Skye, with a lovely old elm and gondola-shaped hazels, all exhibiting the classic response to persistent browsing by producing a trunk-like main stem which has partly collapsed but maintaining a canopy held high above browsing level. Removal of grazing, has led to a characteristic flush of strong basal regeneration.

Peter Quelch

Management suggestions

The Leitir Fura part of the Kinloch and Kyleakin Hills SSSI is known to be one of the lichen 'hotspots' on Skye, mainly for assemblages found on ash, wych elm and hazel. A period of recovery is occurring in areas that were underplanted with conifer, as part of the Plantation on Ancient Woodland Site (PAWS) restoration project, although the hazels pictured bottom left, were not in the affected area. There is potential here for these moribund hazels to assume greater epiphytic lichen cover over time, as it is a site of known high species diversity. The advice would be to allow the hazels to continue to develop 'naturally'. Deer are still present, so a low grazing input is anticipated, perhaps enough to ensure that glades remain open, and that dense closed-canopy thicket development does not occur. Glades are essential, and benefit a wide range of wildlife. At Dundonnell, the story is not so clear; there have obviously been long periods of intensive grazing, when the hazel was severely reduced and almost lost to the wood pasture. Reduction (or removal) of grazing, perhaps 20-30 years ago, enabled partial recovery. Biodiversity is severely reduced, and a period of cessation of grazing would certainly benefit the habitat and the site.

A huge hazel (possibly older than 100 years), on a boundary bank beside a track at Dundonnell, 2007. This site is quite heavily sheep grazed, so basal regeneration is mostly browsed. Dr Brian Coppins examining the *Lobarion* which is well represented on the rough-barked trunks.

Management suggestions

At some stage, this top-heavy shrub may topple onto the track, and need to be cut up and cleared away. Perhaps some remedial management here, such as cutting back some of the larger, leaning stems, may save the tree. If this is done sympathetically, maybe cutting two out of the three stems, and high enough up that regrowth will not be vulnerable to browsing by sheep or deer, then a 'pollard' effect may be achieved. However, it is not known how ancient hazels in this form respond to lopping or pollarding. Some veteran trees that have been re-pollarded after a long period of neglect have not survived the shock of losing significant canopy after cutting. There are no convincing examples of pollarding of the ancient hazels at Dundonnell, so suggesting this as a management option would be purely experimental. Dundonnell contains areas of ancient wood pasture, and is a lichen-rich site, especially on ash. Prolonged grazing by sheep has severely affected the hazel, so that most occur as veteran specimens. This has had a deleterious effect on the lichens of the *Graphidion*, with only rather species-poor assemblages present, although the large, leafy-lobed *Lobarion* community is very well represented, especially on hazel and ash.

Peter Quelch

This superb example of a veteran hazel at Abriachan, Loch Ness-side, 2001, is somewhat outside the limit of oceanicity for Atlantic hazel. The old, thick 'trunks' are over 100cm girth. The new, vigorous regrowth is the result of removal of grazing pressure.

This strange hazel 'tree' at Bruach, Loch Arklet, is another example of hazel persisting in the face of constant browsing. The history of this hazel appears complex; it has obviously been part of a pasture woodland regime for a long time, possibly well over 100 years, so would easily be classified as a 'veteran tree'. The strange twisting of the lower trunk may be an ancient legacy from honeysuckle 'strangling' the stem when it was much younger and perhaps part of a now long-vanished hazelwood (honeysuckle can act like a strangling fig to young hazel stems). The bulky formation at the top of the 'trunk', could suggest a 'bolling', produced by deliberate cutting (pollarding). Alternatively, it could be the effect of breaking-off of large old upper canopy stems, resulting in the present flush of healthy, even-aged stems supporting the canopy. The swollen base is indicative of long periods where basal shoots have been produced, but browsed off. These trees are important for their cultural interest as they give indications or clues about historical management.

Ben Averis

This wonderful old veteran hazel 'tree' is swathed in the tree lungwort *Lobaria pulmonaria*, near Plockton, Wester Ross, 2006.

4. Type D: Hazels in woodland (including ravines)

Hazel is often encountered as a component of semi-natural woodland, but the percentage cover varies enormously, depending on topography and past and present management. As hazel is primarily a pioneer species of open ground, it tends to begin to struggle as competition from taller trees increases. Hazel can be found persisting as small groups forming a mosaic within a woodland, but usually the topography of broken ground will provide opportunity for small groups, or even individual hazels to persist in a robust and viable state. Streams and burns, cutting down through wooded areas, can form small ravines, or localised broad or narrow floodplains, all habitats that may retain a hazel component. Deep ravines tend to be too shaded for hazel to thrive, but sometimes there are more open and better-lit sections where hazel will persist and provide a valuable reservoir of bryophytes or lichens not encountered elsewhere within the habitat.

Examples of hazel in woodlands

A common situation is to find hazel stands in shallow, lowland valleys, with perhaps semi-natural woodland on the slopes above. If there has been a long history of over-grazing by sheep, so that the hazel stand has become reduced and opened up, and this is followed by a period when grazing is either removed or greatly reduced, then birch will rapidly invade between the open hazel stand.

The example above right (unnamed wood by the Allt nan Canan, by Lochcarron, Wester Ross, 2010), is typical of so many 'bits of woodland' in the Scottish Highlands. It is a small, shallow valley site, today flanked on one side by a conifer plantation. The owner uses the wood as a source of firewood, occasionally selecting and cutting out mostly birch. Prior to this, the site was sheep grazed. Today, it is grazed by only a few deer. There are hazel, birch and oak in the wood. The hazels are affected by the maturing birch and the occasional oak, and are being drawn up and losing structural integrity. The biodiversity interest of this site is moderate, in a Scottish Highlands context, with lichen assemblages indicating that 'old-woodland' habitat is present. The dynamics of this site are linked to management, so when there are long periods of intensive grazing, which may coincide with a heavy demand for wood products and firewood, then light levels will be fairly high. Conversely, the other extreme of circumstances occurs when grazing is significantly reduced (or virtually absent) and demand for wood is low, allowing regeneration to flourish and thus reducing light levels.

Unnamed wood by the Allt nan Canan, by Lochcarron, Wester Ross, 2010

Hazel in a well-lit and sheltered situation in the Dundonnell river ravine, Wester Ross, 2008. The smooth bark of hazel here supports several 'old-woodland' lichens of the *Graphidion* community. Generally, hazel in most of the Dundonnell Estate has been subjected to long-term browsing, and the smooth-bark communities have become depleted through loss of continuity of their preferred habitat conditions. So, it is only in such fairly inaccessible places such as the ravines that any significant 'old-woodland' smooth-bark communities are found to be persisting.

Management options for hazel in small mixed woodlands

In many ways, the low level of disturbance described in the example above is sustainable, as it is a localised, pastoral use of the wood. The presence of hazel here will continue so long as the woodland does not become too dense and shaded. The full potential of species associated with pure stands of Atlantic hazel is unlikely to be present, but the hazel will still provide a habitat, as a woody species, for bryophytes, fungi and lichens that would not otherwise be present within the wood.

Hazel is amazingly tenacious and seems able to survive, despite enduring adverse conditions over long periods. Rackham (2003) estimated that hazel might persist under dense shade for 50 years in a southern English wood. Hazel also seems to be able to endure and adapt to long periods of intensive browsing, where sometimes it is reduced to a single tree-like trunk, with a high canopy. When conditions improve, hazel will rapidly revert to its multi-stemmed growth form.

Small ravine woodland, by Lochcarron, Wester Ross, 2010. Hazel in ravines will often grow thickened, elongated stems in order to reach up to the light. The large 'trunk' in the foreground is hazel (covered with the tree lungwort *Lobaria pulmonaria*). Bryophytes and lichens that require relatively high levels of humidity and are shade-tolerant can be a special feature of hazels in ravines. Several very rare species with restricted distribution and habitat niche requirements are known from ravine hazels, the most well known being the lichen blackberries in custard *Pyrenula hibernica*.

John Douglass

Blackberries in custard is a BAP lichen, known only from western Scotland, south-west Ireland, north Wales and Macaronesia. A species of sheltered ravines, this example is from Glasdrum NNR, Argyll, 2007. In Sunart, blackberries in custard has been found on ravine hazel at Resipole SSSI, at Camastorsa (a PAWs Site), amongst conifers. Other sites include Glen Stockdale, Argyll, and on Mull, at Ardura.

Typical Atlantic hazel stand, Nedd, Sutherland 2007.

Atlantic hazel management advice

Atlantic hazel – management

There is a lot of Atlantic hazel that is in 'good' condition, and it is usually obvious by looking at a stand as to whether it is healthy and the structure is being maintained, whether it is either overgrazed and 'exhausted', or whether it is becoming subsumed within a dense, dark and impenetrable thicket. Appendix I provides guidelines for deciding which stand type (or types) your hazelwood may fit into, and how to assess if it is in 'good' or 'poor' condition. It will also enable you to make an assessment of the biodiversity importance of your hazelwood. Broad prescriptions for the appropriate management of hazel are set out here.

Hazel seems to have a remarkable capacity to survive, despite enduring years of unsuitable management. However, for the lichens, bryophytes and fungi associated with and dependent on hazel, the impact of unsuitable management can be profound and can change a stand from one of high diversity to low diversity, sometimes very rapidly, such as when the stand is coppiced. The 'traffic lights table' at the end of this section summarises the range of management practices that are beneficial for Atlantic hazelwoods, and those which are harmful.

The aims of positive management of Atlantic hazelwood habitat are:
● To safeguard and ensure the continuity of the Atlantic hazelwood habitat;

● To provide links or corridors between isolated patches of Atlantic hazel habitat, and by so doing increase and safeguard the viability of the habitat and associated species.

This will be achieved through the development and implementation of management plans that address all of the preceding, but also provide value in terms of return for the landowner and/or grazier.

There are recognised 'core' stands that are known to be important examples of the classic Atlantic hazel habitat. But, equally importantly, there are instances where more recently expanded hazel will enhance existing core stands as well as provide future habitat. So, how do you know if the stands or patches of hazel on your land, or land that you graze, could include 'core' hazelwoods? The guidance provided in Appendix I will help to assess the condition and biodiversity status of your areas of Atlantic hazelwood.

It is important to understand what management is damaging to the hazel habitat.

There are three key activities that will damage the Atlantic hazel habitat:
● Coppicing
● Overgrazing
● No grazing

Coppicing

One of the most damaging management activities for Atlantic hazel is coppicing. Coppicing is cutting all (or nearly all) stems: 'clear-felling' the hazel to leave a coppiced stool. There is a current upsurge of interest in coppicing hazel, both for conservation reasons (Warren *et al.* 2001) and to satisfy an expanding market in coppice products, especially in rural Scotland where hazel is locally plentiful, and initiatives for biofuel from community woodland are being encouraged and funded. Caution is advised before embracing this latest 'good idea' as the practice may not be viable in the long term. Hazelwoods may well be enthusiastically coppiced for one or two cycles, then the practice could fall into abeyance for a variety of reasons (not cost-effective, problems with slow or ragged regrowth, problems with fencing out deer, etc.). The result will be 'neglected coppice', in every sense of the phrase. The

rich assemblage of species – the biodiversity value – characteristic of Atlantic hazelwoods depends on the continuity of hazels for its existence. The risk of allowing coppicing in this habitat is that all the accumulated wildlife interest will be eradicated, and the re-growth will simply be a barren set of stems. Hence, in western Scotland, the precautionary principle is recommended: if there is an overriding desire to 'do something with the hazel scrub', and there is a ready market, then the notion of selective cutting would appear to be the best practice, combining retention of overall habitat ecology with production of a useful end product.

Glen Nant, May 2010, stand Type B, hazel 'trees' developing on a grazed hillside.

Myths or misguided conservation as reasons to coppice

Coppicing is carried out in hazelwoods today for what appear to be genuine conservation reasons:

- A desire to 'rejuvenate old stools'
- Concern that hazel will die out if it is not regularly coppiced
- The belief that coppicing is good for encouraging butterflies and flowers

To rejuvenate old hazels – By cutting old hazels off at the base, the remaining coppice will certainly send up healthy and prolific new stems (so long as deer and other herbivores are kept away). However, it is now recognised that hazel will continually self-perpetuate, particularly if grazing is reduced or removed. Some old hazels may be considered ancient veterans (or, if left to continue, will develop into ancient shrubs), with their special, associated wealth of wildlife, not to mention landscape and cultural history. The worst scenario would be to completely cut down an old hazel, then not protect the exposed base from the attention of deer, so that regeneration is browsed off and the hazel dies.

Hazel will die out if it is not regularly coppiced – This myth probably arises from the mistaken notion that all stands of multi-stemmed hazel are actually 'old hazel coppice', so will need to be coppiced regularly. The fact that hazel has probably been present along the western seaboard of Scotland for nearly 10,000 years indicates that it can obviously continue to live, thrive and spread without being coppiced. Rackham (2003) has described how hazel that was formerly managed as coppice in English woodlands is, indeed, now suffering and beginning to die out, simply because it is being shaded out by a taller tree canopy. There is no regeneration (nut production) of hazel under a shady tree canopy, and the coppice stool becomes weakened from low light levels inhibiting successful basal-shoot establishment.

Coppicing is good for encouraging butterflies and flowers – This may certainly be true in parts of southern England, where coppicing has been practised on a regular basis for hundreds of years; there are references in the Domesday Book to plots of 'underwood', which is the term given to small timber or wood, cut or coppiced on a regular basis. But the land tenure, manors, villages and towns in southern England were intensively managed from early medieval times, when demands (particularly for small wood) were very high. So large woodland holdings were divided into coups, which were cut on a regular rotation (Rackham

2003). Coppicing in coups was, in effect, the creation of periodic glades within a woodland. Flowering plants and butterflies associated with woodland glades were able to flourish in (or, in the case of butterflies, move between) the different coups as they became suitable. As coppicing fell into disuse, glades have closed over and there has been a decline in the richness of the ground flora, and in butterfly populations associated with coppice management. Some experiments were carried out in northern England where stands of hazel (long out of coppice rotation) were re-coppiced in an effort to try to restore floristic diversity and encourage butterflies (Warren *et al.* 2001). Problems mostly centred on keeping roe deer away from regrowth, but although there was some good response from the ground flora, the butterfly populations were too far distant to re-invade the habitat. There also has to be a commitment to continuing the coppice management, perhaps every seven years, in order for a habitat to become established.

Grazing in western Scotland

In western Scotland, the characteristic biodiversity of glades occurs in the generally patchy nature of western woodlands. Woods are often not compartmentalised into discrete blocks, and fenced off, but grade seamlessly into pasture, giving rise to pasture woodlands, occurring naturally as mosaics with open areas, reflecting the topography and soil type. Grazing animals are an important part of this habitat, keeping glades open and thereby maintaining the diversity of the overall habitat, including stands of Atlantic hazel in woodlands, woodland edges, beside streams, etc. Areas of land that were not suitable for cultivation were used for grazing, and depending on the duration and intensity of the flocks and herds, the pasture woodland habitat endured.

However, many overgrazed areas became totally devoid of all trees and shrubs. Husbanding a valuable resource, such as hazel, obviously required controlling animal access, and sometimes remains of old dykes can be found within hazelwoods, especially in association with settlements and small farms. But it is likely that herding or shepherding were the methods most commonly employed to keep animals away from woods at certain times. Hazel was useful for a whole range of necessary products (poles, baskets, pegs, tool handles, etc.), and the hazel rods were harvested by selectively cutting the required stems out of the shrub. Hazelnuts also provided an important food source.

Using woodlands in pastoral landscapes as sheltered grazing has been a long tradition in the west of Scotland, and the Atlantic hazel is a vital element of that tradition. The spring flowers within a stand of ancient hazel that has never been coppiced are spectacular. There were, of course, instances where grazing animals did need to be excluded from woods, the best examples being the oak woods that were regularly coppiced for tan-bark and charcoal.

Selective cutting

Selective cutting is currently practiced by Brian Wilson, a thatcher who runs a small business in Ullapool, specialising in traditional building techniques (Milliken & Bridgewater 2004, pp. 88 & 89): 'One of my favourite plants is hazel, and I always have half an eye open for the long, straight re-growth stems of ancient roadside coppice [sic] groves. It's a superbly versatile material for the construction of anything from "hingin' lum" chimneys to wall panels, partitions and the spars and staples in thatched roofs. To form staples, fresh hazel wands are roasted over a fire to drive the sap away from the middle, twisted briskly then bent over into a springy U-shape and sharpened. It's one of the best jobs for a thatcher on a cold spring day; feet up, twisting sticks over a good fire with a wee dram for company, and the sweet smell of smoked hazel bark hanging in the air.'

(Left) A small rustic gate, made by local farmer Matthew Jeuken from selectively cut hazel stems, to discourage cattle from going down the path to a holy well. The Burren, Co. Clare, south-west Ireland, 2008.

The extensive hazel stands at Leob, on the Ross of Mull, looking north across Loch Scridain towards Ardmeanach and the peak of Bearraich, 2000. Quite dense clusters and stands of pure hazel occur within open areas with bracken and bluebells. These hazel stands are known to have high value for nature, with the hazel gloves fungus present.

Also, the white script lichen occurs here. This is a crustose lichen that has so far not been found anywhere else in the world other than the Atlantic hazelwoods of Western Scotland. It is highly unlikely that these hazels were ever coppiced.

Continuous heavy grazing

Atlantic hazelwoods that suffer from continuous heavy grazing will exhibit some or all of the following features:

- Disruption of the natural processes of the habitat;

- Loss of habitat structure and of young hazels;

- Lack of natural regeneration, as new shoots arising from the base of the hazel are constantly thwarted by browsing;

- Hazels develop unstable growth forms on few stems, with an unnaturally elevated canopy, prone to collapse and wind-blow;

- Ground flora is trampled and poached, and excessive dunging produces unnaturally high levels of nutrient-enrichment;

- Loss of species dependent on continuity of habitat conditions within an old-growth stand; this particularly applies to the crustose lichens of the *Graphidion* community that require the intimacy of continuous cover and regular supply of young, smooth-barked stems. High, elevated canopies of hazel 'trees' do not provide this, being too exposed.

Hazel stands are valued as sheltered grazing, but excessive numbers of livestock gathering in a localised area over winter months can soon degrade the habitat. Here, browsing and breaking off of hazel stems, and trampling by cattle are clearly a problem, and a period of recovery is urgently required.

Hazel woodland under continuous grazing, reduced to a few gnarled, scattered individuals, most as single-trunked hazel 'trees' with high canopies. These 'trees' will have lost the characteristic niches that the specialised lichens require. They will still retain some biodiversity value, but unless grazing is reduced, their future is uncertain.

David Genney

Acton/Griffith

Long-term exclosure from all grazing

Exclosure of an area of woodland is generally undertaken to halt decline in woodland structure by removing large herbivores in order to allow uninhibited tree and shrub regeneration, the so-called 'natural regeneration.' The problem for the habitat arises when the exclosure fence is left up for an extended period after the desired regeneration has established, and the woodland becomes a dense, shaded and impenetrable thicket. Exclosure encourages regeneration not only of the trees and shrubs, but also of other palatable plants such as bramble and ivy. The closing-up of glades, the reduction of light and increase in dank humidity ultimately leads to an overall lowering and loss of biodiversity. The importance of woodland glades for a whole range of organisms, including butterflies, flies, birds, flowering plants and lichens has already been described.

At the site below, two extremes of management can be seen. In the foreground is heavily sheep-grazed pasture, with a few isolated hazel 'trees'. The swollen bases of the hazel trunks indicate that the annual production of basal shoots has been constantly browsed off, resulting in this characteristic swelling. The tenacity of hazel to survive in the face of constant browsing is clearly demonstrated here, with dead birch trunks littering the ground in between the hazels.

In the background, behind the deer fence, is the other extreme: a long-term exclosure with a mass of regeneration, now assuming dense, shaded thicket proportions. The deer fence needs to be lowered to stock-proof height, to allow occasional deer into the dense woodland in the hope of re-establishing some glades and generally opening up the woodland to light.

Acton/Griffith

Summary of management practices that will have harmful, neutral or beneficial effects on the Atlantic hazelwood habitat.

Management that will have serious negative impacts on Atlantic Hazel habitats	
Management action	**Result**
Coppicing	Disrupts natural processes of the habitat; all lichens, fungi and bryophytes growing on the hazel will be removed with the cut stems
	Destroys ecological continuity, resulting in loss of species dependent on this, e.g. mostly crustose lichens of the *Graphidion* community, but also the larger, leafy-lobed lichens of the *Lobarion* community
	Removes shade and reduces humidity, to the detriment of species that rely on these conditions, e.g. Oceanic bryophytes
	Reduces fungal diversity
Continuous heavy grazing	Disrupts natural processes of the habitat, and leads to loss of habitat structure, loss of hazel
	Natural regeneration by producing new shoots from the base is constantly thwarted by grazing
	Hazels develop unstable growth forms on few stems, with an unnaturally elevated canopy, prone to wind-blow
	Ground flora is trampled and poached, and excessive dunging produces nutrient-enriched conditions
	Loss of species dependent on continuity of habitat conditions within an old-growth stand
Long-term exclosures	Can disrupt natural processes of the habitat by excluding occasional light grazing; this leads to a loss of glades and build-up of rank vegetation
	The gladed edges to hazel stands are compromised and lost to dense, thicket regeneration
'Scrub' clearance	Destroys the habitat
Unsuitable siting of cattle feeding stations	Localised intensive use of areas of Atlantic hazel will result in ground flora being trampled and poached, and excessive dunging produces unnaturally high levels of nutrient-enrichment
Rhododendron ponticum	Invasion by this non-native evergreen shrub results in a general loss of biodiversity, through the effects of over-shading and toxic leachate from the leaf-litter

Management that will not damage Atlantic hazel habitats, or will have minimum impact if guidelines are followed	
Selective cutting of stems	A more ecologically sensitive and sympathetic way of harvesting stems from Atlantic hazel; selective cutting enables the internal integrity of individual hazels to be maintained (together with their associated biodiversity), and the cohesion of the stand as an ecological unit.
Short periods of intensive grazing	Atlantic hazel has a natural ability to respond to overgrazing for short periods, but extended continuous heavy grazing reduces viability of the individual hazels and the stand.
Short periods of no grazing	A respite period from grazing results in a general thickening-up of the stand, and can be useful to allow recovery from periods when overgrazing may have reduced viability within the stand; however, subsequent reintroduction of grazing at low to moderate levels is recommended to keep glades open.

Management that will preserve and enhance Atlantic hazel habitats	
Light seasonal grazing	Light grazing will ensure glades are kept open, an important habitat feature that benefits a range of wildlife within the hazel habitat; there may be some slight damage to stems, and some basal regeneration will be browsed, but the level should be sustainable.
Re-introduction of grazing into hazel stands that were formerly fenced to exclude all grazing	This must be a gradual process, i.e. domestic animals must have access to easy bite as well as struggling through thickets, where animal welfare may be compromised. The aim would be to restore glades within a stand that had closed up into thicket regeneration.
Encourage hazel expansion	Managing grazing to enable isolated hazel stands or widely spaced clumps to form an integrated habitat (without compromising glade or woodland-edge habitats). Needs to be carefully managed.
Planting hazel to replenish a severely reduced habitat	Using hazelnuts locally sourced and carefully propagated in a nursery (protected from mice and vole predation), and planted out as well-established saplings, initially protected by Tuley tubes, has been successfully carried out, e.g. at Taynish NNR.

Appendix

Atlantic hazel canopy in full leaf, Luing, July 2010

Atlantic hazel site assessment

 Determining the Atlantic hazel stand type present (using the key to Hazel stand types, below)

As Atlantic hazel can cover a wide range of stand types, growth forms and management histories, a site assessment needs to be attempted in order to identify and quantify the range of possible stand types, to evaluate their condition and to assess their biodiversity value.

Four main hazel stand types (incorporating various growth forms of hazel) are identified. There is usually a need to distinguish between stand types before giving appropriate management advice. There may be one clearly defined hazel stand type, **but it is more likely that there will be several of the following, blending together, or as mosaics amongst other habitats.**

All types have *potential* to be important for biodiversity.

Closed canopy, multi-stemmed stands of pure hazel	**Type A**
Scattered hazels in pasture	**Type B**
Veteran hazels	**Type C**
Hazel in woodland (including ravines)	**Type D**

Key to Atlantic hazel stand types

1   Closed canopy, multi-stemmed stands dominated by hazel; sometimes difficult to walk between the individual hazels 2

   Open canopy, individual hazel shrubs variously spaced, sometimes in small clumps with open, grazed areas between; easy to walk between them 4

2   Closed canopy, multi-stemmed stands dominated by hazel; sometimes difficult to walk between the shrubs . . . . **Type A**

   Closed canopy, mostly multi-stemmed stands of hazel, but other woody species (e.g. birch, oak, ash, holly, rowan, etc.) present 3

3   Closed canopy, mostly multi-stemmed stands of hazel, but other woody species present but comprising < 25% of the overall stand . . . . **Type A**

   Closed canopy, mostly multi-stemmed stands of hazel, but other woody species present but comprising > 25% of the overall stand (this also applies to hazel in ravines) 5

4   Hazel in small clumps or scattered mosaics, or widely spaced; can be present as multi-stemmed forms, or with few stems to each hazel and occasionally 'tree-like'; other tree/shrub species may/may not be present as rare/occasional; in open, grazed mosaics, sometimes with bracken. . . . . **Type B***

   Hazel present mostly as a few veterans of considerable size and age; can be at edge of woodlands, or in open, brackeny slopes as a component of an old wood pasture habitat. . **Type C***

5   Closed canopy (although there may be gaps in some situations where glades are present) with hazel present as a component of more mixed deciduous woodland; hazels mostly multi-stemmed, but often few stems in each shrub and tending to be gangly and drawn up . . . . **Type D**

   Hazels in ravines . . . . **Type D**

   Combinations of all of the above can be found, or at least mosaics of varying patches of Types A, B & D (Type C is fairly distinctive, but may be part of Types B & D)

   * Types B & C: an intermediate stage between Type B and the giant veteran hazel forms of Type C would be hazel 'trees'. See examples illustrated in Chapter 5.

Make a brief description of the area(s) of hazel you wish to assess:

e.g. 'along lower edge of slope, backing on to grazed fields above, and shaded burn below – hazel stands quite open with scattered old bushes; canopy closed in some places, but forming open gladed mosaics. Typically with few hazels having up to about 20 stems, with little evidence of young shoots establishing. Hazel gloves seen on a couple of bushes. Occasional hawthorn present, with willow around burn. Grazed by sheep all year round. (Type B).'

Name of site:
Brief description of the hazel area(s)

Now try to fit your hazel stand(s) into the **Hazel Assessment Table 1 (HAT.1)**. If you have more than one example of any type, then make that clear, e.g. 'Type A present in three places (with approx. grid references); Type B scattered and wide-spread throughout the holding.' If it is easier or clearer, use separate copies of **HAT.1** (see **http://www.snh.gov.uk/docs/B797477.pdf** for more copies of the Tables).

Table HAT.1 **Atlantic Hazel Structure Types**	Present (grid ref(s))	Approx area (or for Type C, give number of shrubs)
Type A: closed canopy, multi-stemmed stands dominated by hazel		
Type B: scattered hazels in pasture (including occasional 'tree' hazels)		
Type C: veteran hazels		
Type D: Hazels in woodland (including ravines)		

Atlantic hazel habitat condition

Having identified which hazel stand types may be present, the next step is to attempt to assess the condition of the habitat. 'Condition' is, to some extent, an emotive word, and it is certainly not clear-cut as to what distinguishes 'good' condition from 'poor' condition. The terms 'favourable condition' and 'unfavourable condition' have specific meanings within the context of SNH's Site Condition Monitoring (SCM) guidelines. The following habitat condition assessment is distinct from SNH's SCM assessment process, although should inform the development of SCM targets for designated sites with this woodland feature. In order to avoid confusion or conflict, the terms 'favourable' and 'unfavourable' are not used, but 'good' and 'poor' are substituted. In Chapter 5, examples of hazel in good and poor condition in different structure types are illustrated and described.

 Determining whether the various Atlantic hazel stand types on your land are in 'good' or 'poor' condition.

Table HAT.2 is a broad-brush method to enable an assessment of the different hazel stands you may have. Use a separate sheet if there is more than one example of each type (see **http://www.snh.gov.uk/docs/B797477.pdf** for more copies of the Tables).

Table HAT.2 Atlantic Hazel Condition Assessment	Yes Score 1	No Score 0
Type A (closed canopy, multi-stemmed stands of pure hazel)		
Closed canopy mostly intact (apart from some occasional glades)		
Hazels often fairly small, evenly-spaced, with usually slender to medium-sized stems (c. 3-25cm girth)		
Ground flora not (or only slightly) trampled, with few bare areas or just occasional tracks/paths		
Stems mottled with bryophytes and lichens		
Light, seasonal grazing, or grazing by a few deer, with evidence of some basal shoots being browsed		
In 20 hazels, there are at least four instances of a successful young shoot (whip) reaching (or nearly reaching) the canopy, i.e. one hazel in five demonstrates viable growth dynamics within the stand, even with low grazing levels		
Any additional comments:		
Total score for Type A (max = 6)		

Table HAT.2 Atlantic Hazel Condition Assessment	Yes Score 1	No Score 0
Type B (Scattered hazels in pasture including occasional small hazel 'trees')		
Most scattered hazels robust, with many stems of varying thickness, and canopy wide-spreading		
Ground flora not (or only slightly) trampled, with few bare areas or just occasional tracks/paths		
If hazels are reduced to a few thickened stems, are there signs of recovery, with viable, well-established regeneration present (on at least one hazel in five)?		
Stems mottled with bryophytes and lichens		
Light seasonal grazing, or grazing by a few deer, with evidence of a few basal shoots being browsed		
Any additional comments:		
Total score for Type B (max = 5)		
Type C (veteran hazels, or veteran hazel 'trees')	**Yes**	**No**
How many veteran hazels are present within the site? (score 1 point under the YES column for each veteran)		
Do the veteran hazel 'trees' appear viable, i.e. at least some viable canopy present above grazing height? (score 1 point for each veteran)		
Trunk(s) is/are stable, and not requiring pruning (score 1 point for each)		
If in imminent danger of collapse, is there potential for remedial pruning/pollarding, in order to preserve the hazel? (score 1 point for each veteran where this action would be applicable)		
Trunks with bryophytes and lichens present (score 1 for yes)		
Are the veterans within a pasture woodland habitat today? (score 1 for yes)		
Any additional comments:		
Total score for Type C (min = 5)		

Appendix

Table HAT.2 Atlantic Hazel Condition Assessment	Yes Score 1	No Score 0
Type D (Hazel in woodland, including ravines)		
Hazels forming discrete mosaics amongst other tree species (e.g. at streamsides)		
Glades present		
Individual hazels not widely separated (isolated) from other hazels, i.e. not more than 20m apart		
Hazels not reduced to one or two stems only		
Hazels not becoming tall and gangly, drawn up by being shaded from increased canopy development or infill from taller tree species (unless in ravines)		
Ground flora not (or only slightly) trampled, with few bare areas, or just occasional tracks/paths		
Stems mottled with bryophytes and lichens		
Evidence of light seasonal grazing within the woodland, or grazing by a few deer, so that at least some basal shoots are noted as successfully getting away to maintain viability of the hazel(s) (at least one in five)		
Any additional comments:		
Total score for Type D (max = 8)		
HAT.2. Total Score For All Hazel Types Present		

6

What clues can you use to assess if the hazel stand is likely to have high biodiversity value?

Determining the biodiversity importance of the Atlantic hazel stand

To make a decision about the biodiversity value of the hazel stand calls for assessment of some features that are clues as to whether the stand supports at least some of the key features special to Atlantic hazel. Look for the species described below. Note that apart from **hazel gloves** and **glue fungus**, **there is no need to name any bryophyte or lichen**, but just look and see to what extent they are present. The following are just examples to give you some idea of what's around.

Examples of the fungus hazel gloves *Hypocreopsis rhododendri*, a strong indicator of hazel stands of high biodiversity importance. This fungus has a hard, rubbery texture, and cannot be confused with anything else growing on hazel. The example at lower right, shows the fungus in a senescent state, so it looks greyish and woody, although there are characteristic orange lobes at the outer edges. The upper surface has been extensively browsed by slugs or snails.

Dave Genney, 2007

Examples of the **glue fungus** *Hymenochaete corrugata* trapping dead twigs fallen from the upper canopy. Circled areas (left) show points of attachment; this little fallen hazel twig is firmly glued in two places where it touches other hazel stems.

The photograph left shows a medium-sized dead hazel twig, lodged and stuck with the glue fungus against fairly small twigs.

Sometimes it is difficult to actually see the glue fungus, but giving potential fallen twigs a little tweak will soon indicate if they are 'glued'.

The photograph bottom left, clearly shows the dark brown glue fungus holding twigs in place.

There may be more than one species of glue fungus lurking in the Atlantic hazelwoods. This robust example (below) is from Argyll. The thin hazel stems are firmly glued to a much thicker section of dead hazel stem.

The glue fungi belong to a group that digests dead wood; so, by trapping fallen twigs within the shrub, they store up a 'larder' of dead sticks. This avoids competition from other wood-digesting fungi that live on the floor of the woodland. It is believed that hazel gloves is closely associated with at least one of the glue fungi.

Dave Genney

Peter Quelch

Examples of crustose lichens found on the smooth bark of hazel: (right), mini-warts of *Thelotrema petractoides*, (far right) black-spots of *Pyrenula occidentalis*. Below, typical mixed mosaics of small crustose lichens. **You don't have to put names to any of these crustose lichens**; just look closely at smooth hazel bark and spot the patterns.

Examples of leafy-lobed lichens found on hazel: (above left), octopus suckers *Collema fasciculare*, and (above right) yellow specklebelly *Pseudocyphellaria crocata*.

Above: Typical leafy-lobed lichens from Atlantic hazel: old hazel stems laden with the green tree lungwort *Lobaria pulmonaria*, plus a couple of grey-lobed lichens.

Left: Old hazel stems totally covered with lichens. Here, there is the parchment lichen or *Lobaria amplissima* (pale, yellowish-green lobes, which do go a perfect parchment cream when dry), and the western plum lichen *Degelia cyanoloma*. A couple of other lichens are also squeezed in on the branch.

10

Gordon Rothero

Examples of bryophytes found on hazel in Atlantic hazelwoods.
From the left: toothed pouncewort *Drepanolejeunea hamatifolia*, Killarney featherwort
Plagiochila bifaria, frizzled pin-cushion *Ulota phyllantha*.

An older hazel, with good cover of green mosses, as well as leafy-lobed lichens.

A young hazel stem, with brown and green bryophytes, and whitish crustose lichens.

Two common bryophytes found on Atlantic hazel:

Far left: the frizzled pin-cushion, a neat, spiky-looking moss.

Left: the delicate red-brown fronds of a scalewort; this is a 'leafy liverwort' and is very common in Atlantic hazelwoods.

11

Table HAT.3 enables a fairly broad-brush assessment of the biodiversity value of the Atlantic hazel (mostly applicable to Type A, but also can be used for Types B and D). Use a separate Table HAT.3 for each patch of hazel you are assessing, as there may be significant differences between stands (see **http://www.snh.gov.uk/docs/B797477.pdf** for more copies of the Tables). Score 3 points for some; score 5 points for plenty (a subjective decision, but probably acceptable if you use common sense).

Table HAT.3 Atlantic Hazel Biodeversity Assessment	None 0	Some 3	Plenty 5
The smooth bark on young stems: does it have patches of crustose lichens, seen as whitish, creamy, silvery, greenish or brownish areas (often with dark dots or dashes), forming mosaics on the bark?			
Are there bryophytes (mosses and liverworts) on the stems?			
Are some of the leafy-lobed lichens present on the stems?*			
Is the hazel gloves fungus present?			
Is the glue fungus present?			
Any additional comments:			
HAT. 3 Total (max = 25)			

*There are some excellent leaflets produced by Plantlife which illustrate the sort of lichens you are likely to see in Atlantic hazelwoods. We suggest buying a laminated copy, as although downloading the pdf. is free, the format is larger than A4. (See *Lichens of the Atlantic Woodlands Guide 1*.
http://www.plantlife.org.uk/uk/plantlife-scotland-publications.html)

12

Results (summary of HAT.1, HAT.2 & HAT.3)

Table HAT.4 – Summary of Atlantic Hazel Resource

Sum of all Atlantic hazel present on the holding (from Table HAT.1)	Approx. area included	Number of individual patches of hazel (or number of hazels of Type C) Count 1 for each individual number of patches, or 1 for each veteran hazel of Type C
Type A (closed canopy, multi-stemmed stands)		
Type B (scattered hazel in pasture)		
Type C (veteran hazels)		
Type D (hazel in woodland, including ravines)		
These totals are simply a summary of the total hazel resource, and are not be added to the condition assessment and biodiversity assessment scores below.		

Table HAT.5 – Summary of Atlantic Hazel Assessment

Atlantic Hazel Habitat Condition Assessment (from Table HAT.2)	
Total score Type A	
Total score Type B	
Total score Type C	
Total score Type D	
Overall total score for habitat condition assessment	
Atlantic Hazel Biodiversity Assessment (from Table HAT.3)	
Overall total score for biodiversity assessment	
Grand Total of Score	

What do these results mean?

The Hazel Assessment Tables (HATs) are an effort to assess the habitat condition and biodiversity importance of individual stands of Atlantic hazel. They are, of necessity, a rather broad-brush approach, as invariably no single stand of hazel will conform to one simple stand type category, but often they will be a blending of several stand types. The scores are a guide only, with the **Threshold score** being set as the minimum to indicate that a particular stand type may have potential as a stand of high biodiversity value.

Hazel stand types	Threshold score	Maximum score
Type A HAT.2 + HAT.3	14	31
Type B HAT.2 + HAT.3	13	30
Type C HAT.2 + HAT.3	14	31+
Type D HAT.2 + HAT.3	15	33
These scores are derived from combining HAT.2 and HAT.3, as shown below:		
Atlantic Habitat Condition HAT.2		
Type A	5	6
Type B	4	5
Type C (veterans)	5	6+
Type D	6	8
Atlantic Hazel Biodiversity Assessment HAT.3	9	25

The purpose of this exercise is to discover potentially species-rich stands of Atlantic hazel, and to encourage sympathetic management, or at least to avoid the worst of unsympathetic management, by simply raising awareness. **The Threshold score of 9 for Biodiversity Assessment (HAT.3) is really the most important.**

The next step:

Either you or your advisor should contact Gordon Gray Stephens (Atlantic Hazel Action Group (AHAG): Gordon Gray Stephens, tel. 01852 500366. info@AtlanticHazel.org).

Gordon will advise whether you need to seek specialist advice to make a simple 'dip-in' visit to confirm the results of the Biodiversity Assessment. The results will be taken into account when seeking to put together an application for funding support from agri-environment schemes or entry into the Woodland Grazing initiative, http://www.forestry.gov.uk/woodlandgrazingtoolbox

14

References

Alireza, G., Me, G., Talaie, A. & Vezvaie, A. 2004. Studies in self-incompatibility alleles in some progenies of hazelnut (*Corylus avellana* L.) using fluorescence microscope. *International Journal of Agriculture and Biology*, 6(1): 113–115.

Averis, A.M., Averis, A.B.G., Birks, H.J.B., Horsfield, D., Thompson, D.B.A. & Yeo, M.J.M. 2004. *An illustrated guide to upland vegetation.* JNCC.

Averis, A.B.G., Hodgetts, N.G., Rothero, G.P. & Genney, D. 2011. *Bryological assessment for hydro-electric schemes in the west Highlands.* Scottish Natural Heritage Commissioned Report No. 449.

Birks, H.J.B. 1989. Holocene isochrone maps and patterns of tree-spreading in the British Isles. *Journal of Biogeography* 16: 503–540.

Coppins, A.M. & Coppins, B.J. 1999. *Report of a visit to Torrin hazel woods, Skye, to assess proposed management options with regard to the lichen interest.* Unpublished report for Highland Birchwoods (for the John Muir Trust).

Coppins, A.M. & Coppins, B.J. 2000a. *Ballachuan Hazelwood SWT Reserve, Argyll Main (VC 98): Lichen Survey II.* Unpublished report for Scottish Wildlife Trust.

Coppins, A.M. & Coppins, B.J. 2000b. *Lichens of Eigg (VC 104 North Ebudes).* Unpublished report for the Scottish Wildlife Trust.

Coppins, A.M. & Coppins, B.J. 2000c. *Mull: investigation of selected hazelwoods for three BAP species: the lichens* Arthothelium macounii *and* Graphis alboscripta *and the fungus* Hypocreopsis rhododendri. Unpublished report for Scottish Natural Heritage and Royal Botanic Garden, Edinburgh.

Coppins, A., Coppins, B. & Quelch, P. 2002. Atlantic hazelwoods: some observations on the ecology of this neglected habitat from a lichenological perspective. *British Wildlife* 14(1): 17–26.

Gilbert, O.L. 1984 Some effects of disturbance on the lichen flora of oceanic hazel woodlands. *Lichenologist* 16: 21–30.

Gulliver, S. 2002. *Spatial Patterns of Genotypic Diversity in Hazel* (Corylus avellana L.). MSc Thesis, University of Edinburgh & Royal Botanic Garden, Edinburgh.

Hæggeström, C.A. 2000. The age and size of hazel (*Corylus avellana* L.) stools of Nåtö Island, Åland Islands, SW Finland. In: M. Agnoletti & S. Anderson (eds), *Methods and Approaches in Forest History* pp. 47–57. Wallingford, CAB International.

McVean, D.N. 1964 Pre-history and ecological history. In: J.H. Burnett (ed), *The Vegetation of Scotland*: 561-567. Oliver & Boyd, Edinburgh & London.

Meteorological Office 1952. *Climatological atlas of the British Isles.* Meteorological Office, London.

Milliken, W. & Bridgewater, S. 2004. *Flora Celtica.* pp. 88–89.Birlinn

Mortimer, S.R., Turner, A.J., Brown, V.K., Fuller, R.J., Good, J.E.G., Bell, S.A., Stevens, P.A., Norris, D., Bayfield, N. & Ward, L.K. 2000. The Nature Conservation Value of Scrub in Britain. *JNCC Report* No. 308.

Preston, C.D., Pearman, D.A. & Dines, T.D. (eds) 2002. *New Atlas of the British and Irish Flora.* Oxford University Press.

Rackham, Oliver 2003 (New Edition). *Ancient Woodland, its history, vegetation and uses in England* Castelpoint Press.

Ratcliffe, D.A. 1968. An ecological account of Atlantic bryophytes in the British Isles. *New Phytologist*, 67: 365–439.

Rhind, P. 2003. Comment: Britain's contribution to global conservation and our coastal temperate rainforest. *British Wildlife*: 15(2): 97–102.

Rodwell, J.S. (ed.) 1991 *British Plant Communities. Volume 1 Woodlands and scrub.* Cambridge University Press.

Rose, F. 1976. Lichenological indicators of age and environmental continuity in woodlands. In: D.H. Brown, D.L. Hawksworth & R.H. Bailey (eds) *Lichenology: Progress and Problems* pp. 278-307. Academic Press, London.

Rose, F. 1992. Temperate Forest Management: its effects on lichen and bryophyte floras and habitats. In: J.W. Bates & A.M. Farmer (eds) *Bryophytes and Lichens in a Changing Environment.* pp.211-233. Oxford University Press.

Tallantire, P.A. 2002 The early Holocene spread of hazel (*Corylus avellana* L.) in Europe north and west of the Alps: an ecological hypothesis. *The Holocene* 12: 91-106.

Tansley, A.G. 1949 *The British Islands and their Vegetation.* pp 471–474. Cambridge University Press.

Warren, M., Clarke, S. & Currie, F. 2001. The Coppice for Butterflies challenge. *British Wildlife* 13: 21–28.

Woods, R.G. & Coppins, B.J. 2003. *A Conservation Evaluation of British Lichens.* British Lichen Society.

Acknowledgements

So many people have contributed to this book that it is impossible to thank them all. Particular acknowledgement must, however, be given to Kate Holl (SNH) for keeping this project alive over several years, until this final fruition. Another main player in getting the project to completion was David Genney (SNH), who was also largely responsible for engineering a version of the book onto Scottish Natural Heritage's website:
http://www.snh.gov.uk/about-scotlands-nature/habitats-and-ecosystems/woodland/atlantic-hazel/

Original input was from several sources, from various experts such as Liz Holden (fungi) and Ben Averis (flowering plants and bryophytes). Contributions to early drafts, particularly by Peter Quelch (on management), Richard Thompson (FE) and Kate Holl (SNH) have been largely incorporated. Useful comments from Stephen Ward helped keep us on track, and Sharon Parr shared her experiences of Atlantic hazel on the Burren. Gordon Rothero (bryophytes) added some useful extras. I am extremely grateful to Andrew Branson and the team at *British Wildlife* for taking on the task of editing the work, and keeping up my flagging spirits with encouraging words. Thanks also go to Gordon Gray Stephens for some stimulating discussions and seeing the project towards completion, and to Helen Meek for her skill and patience in putting the final copy together.

Thanks also go to John Birks, Bergen, for permission to reproduce his isochrone map for *Corylus avellana* in the British Isles (Birks 1989) and to Alison and Ben Averis for permission to use the map showing the climatic oceanicity of the British Isles (Averis *et al.* 2004). This book will be one of the last fruits of Scottish Native Woods. They will be missed.

Finally, we would also like to mention our appreciation of the continuing support, interest and encouragement from Donald Rice of Dundonnell Estate, Wester Ross.

Funding

This book is part of the Atlantic Hazelwood Action Group (AHAG) project, funded by Scottish Natural Heritage; Argyll and the Islands Leader EU Project, and the British Lichen Society.

Photographic credits

I am very grateful to all who have willingly and enthusiastically contributed images: Andy Acton, Ben Averis, John Douglass, Carl Farmer (http://www.nature-diary.co.uk/argyll.htm), Dave Genney, Mary Gibby, Anna Griffith, Liz Holden, Anand Prasad, Peter Quelch, Gordon Rothero, Neil Sanderson and Gordon Gray Stephens.

All unaccredited photos are Sandy and/or Brian Coppins.

Index